THE TRUTH ABOUT PROBATE
AND
FAMILY FINANCIAL PLANNING

How to Build and Preserve
Your Wealth

by

WILLIAM J. CASEY
of the New York Bar

Institute for Business Planning, Inc.
2 W. 13th STREET, NEW YORK, N.Y. 10011

This publication is designed to provide accurate and authoritative information in regard to the subject matter covered. It is sold with the understanding that the publisher is not engaged in rendering legal, accounting or other professional service. If legal advice or other expert assistance is required, the services of a competent professional person should be sought.

— *From a Declaration of Principles jointly adopted by a Committee of the American Bar Association and a Committee of Publishers and Associations.*

© Copyright MCMLXVII by

Institute for Business Planning, Inc.

Third Printing, May 1967

Library of Congress Catalog Card Number: 67-17055

WHAT THIS BOOK DOES

This book is about your future and your family's. It should help you think about your money, your retirement, your family needs, with and without you, and what you must do to see that those needs are satisfied. It's about how to accumulate and protect capital, how to pass it on to your family, how to keep it available for family needs now and in the future.

The one thing I most want this book to do is to put the many phases of family financial planning in proper perspective. Avoiding probate is not good planning, nor is saving taxes. They are merely steps in family financial planning, and not the most important steps either. It's very bad planning to transfer property to avoid probate or save taxes and then discover that you need the property and can't get it—or have your children find that you've locked property up in trust so tightly that it can't be made available to educate them or start them in business.

True financial planning has to focus on the needs of individuals—you, your wife, your children. It must always preserve flexibility to adapt to changing situations. Only after property has been protected and made available to meet changing needs, do tax saving and expense saving become proper objectives.

I believe this book will be valuable *to the layman and to the professional man* as well. It should help the layman to formulate his objectives. It should help him to identify the special problems with respect to each person in his family and each item of his property so that he can and will get the needed professional advice and properly relate it to what he seeks for his family and his property. All advice and all evaluations lead to policy decisions and only the owner of wealth can make these decisions. But he should not make them without experienced and qualified legal and financial advice.

This book is intended to provide a panorama of the available methods of arranging and transferring property. At the same time, it strongly warns against leaping at any panacea—indeed, against adopting any mode of ownership or transfer without having an experienced professional man not only advise but take responsibility for carrying it out.

Some half a million Americans have recently purchased a set of homemade forms in a book which tells them to transfer to another person under a revocable trust every sort of property from an automobile to a portfolio of securities. As spelled out in these pages of mine, the revocable trust is one of a dozen methods of transferring property to your family. It is a valuable and effective method where it fits. The American Bar Association has produced and has, for some time, been circulating a film which spells out what can be accomplished by transferring title to property to a revocable trust. Lawyers generally make use of the revocable trust. Banks and life insurance people bring this method of property transfer to the attention of property owners.

But a property owner is short changed unless he has this method of property transfer evaluated *in his particular circumstances* against all the other methods of transfer (and combinations of them) which are spelled out in these pages.

Every time anybody buys stock or real estate, takes out insurance, changes jobs or puts money in the bank, he is estate planning in a fashion. But it's almost always haphazard. Money is dissipated unnecessarily, opportunities are lost, the family is exposed to unanticipated hazards. This book seeks to show you not only how you can build and transfer your property most advantageously, but also what liabilities must be provided for, how they can be minimized and paid, and what will be left for your family. It then deals with the available ways to increase and protect the capital available for you and your family. All this is for the purpose of helping you find out where you stand, giving you ideas as to how you might improve your situation and stimulating you to get professional advice on whether these ideas will work for you, and professional help in adapting those that fit you to your particular family and financial circumstances.

FOR THE PROFESSIONAL MAN

I hope and believe this book will *help the professional estate planner* also. From experience, I know that the most critical and difficult part of the estate planning art is to get the needs, the assets and the desires of a family in proper and meaningful perspective. Then, there is the problem of presenting and interpreting the future to them, showing them what will happen to family capital and income under the combined impact of the provisions of wills and trusts, the probate procedure and the tax laws.

I hope this book enables the professional to check the methods and perspectives he has developed against those which I have found useful . . . and to borrow those elements which he likes as I have from so many of my professional colleagues, who have shared their experiences in working on matters together and in panel discussions held for the edification of the profession.

Finally, I have described what I consider the cardinal sins of estate planning and listed a large number of specific pit- falls which can frustrate the best laid plans but which are more likely to occur to the unplanned, unadvised and canned estate. All of us who carry the responsibility of planning for the future of families live in dread of such pitfalls, and I trust this catalogue will be both reassuring and useful.

I would like to thank Bert Westlin and Carl Paffendorf for helping me prepare this book.

William J. Casey

TABLE OF CONTENTS

CHAPTER XVIII—HOW TO TRANSFER THE MOST AT DEATH

CHAPTER XIX—WHAT YOUR WILL SHOULD DO

CHAPTER XX—HOW TO PICK YOUR PERSONAL REPRESENTATIVE

CHAPTER XXI—SINS AND PITFALLS

APPENDIX

CHAPTER I

HOW TO THINK ABOUT YOUR ESTATE

A layman—you—has to plan your estate. Even if you're a lawyer, you function as a layman when you plan your own estate. You must evaluate the strengths, weaknesses, and needs of your beneficiaries; only you make the policy decisions—who gets what and when. Everyone needs a lawyer to advise on the legal opportunities and pitfalls. Lawyers, bankers, insurance and investment advisers, and accountants can draw on their experience and contribute technical knowledge, financial analysis, and perspective to your planning. A lawyer must implement the plan and advise your heirs in carrying it out when death does occur. But *only you can decide what your family needs and how your property and earning power can be marshalled to meet those needs now and in the future.*

The best estate planning advice I've heard comes from a layman, Charles A. Mott, one of the founders of the General Motors Corporation, now an octogenarian philanthropist. He says, "I certainly know of no finer or surer way of assuring the best results than for *a man to figure that he has died* and then to *figure out what he would have to do as executor.* If he uses ordinary intelligence and also calls upon the assistance of others qualified to overcome the difficulties which he unearths, he certainly could do a better job for his family."

He goes into further detail:

"Consider that I passed away last night. This morning, as executor for the fellow who died last night, I take over affairs. I read the will and its various provisions, etc., and I also make a list of all the assets which have to be considered for disposal.

Has there been sufficient insurance or other provision to

1

take care of the family and beneficiaries? Is insurance carried to finance taxes?

If so, is it certain that the proceeds will be available for this purpose when needed?

Has the deceased left his personal affairs in a jumbled-up state or with proper records and proper provisions for liquidating obligations and inheritance taxes? A thorough analysis is necessary.

And then would I, as executor, discover a tremendous number of things that I, the businessman, should have done before I passed out, and a great many things that should have been done differently? And would I, as executor, wish to Heaven that I could call myself, the individual, back to life for at least one day so that I could do the things that I should have done before passing out?"

Your estate has two jobs to do: give you independence and security while you live and give your family independence and security after you die. It is not merely something you will leave behind some day. You have a lot more to think about than the mechanics and the cost of transferring your property to your family. That's important but not nearly as important as seeing that your estate is set up to accomplish its two jobs.

Some 300,000 Americans have recently bought a book that may create the impression that probate is necessarily bad and any scheme to evade probate is necessarily good. The fact is that a good estate plan is one that creates the maximum benefits for the right beneficiaries. A bad plan is one that does anything less. Probate or no probate is simply an incidental question. The answer falls into place naturally and properly when your affairs are placed in the hands of a competent lawyer. His fees are a small premium to pay to insure the proper protection of your beneficiaries.

Most people never achieve full independence and security

in the sense that they can forget about working and can rely entirely on the property they have accumulated. But even a year's income stashed away represents a degree of independence and security, and that's the only true meaning your savings have. Once you understand this, several things follow:

(1) As much of your estate as possible should be in assets that are not related to your business and do not otherwise depend on you. You should try to get free assets that will produce income without you.

(2) The best plan for your estate is one that assumes you are dead and sets up your property now as closely as possible to the way you would want to have it set up for your family. Try to be your own executor.

(3) Set an estate objective that, with Social Security and other available income, will produce the living money your family needs—both when you retire and when you die. This should be the measure and target of your insurance and investment program.

(4) On paper, work out what will happen to your property when you die; how it will be applied to pay debts, taxes, and expenses; what will be left and how much income that amount will produce each year for your family. Your estate plan is a program to increase and protect the assets and income left for your family without significantly impairing your flexibility to change your mind and adapt to the needs and circumstances that emerge during your remaining life.

This book is a modest effort to interest you in developing such a plan and help you approach it.

The first thing you need is a sounding board—someone to talk things over with, to try ideas on, to get reactions from. This may be your wife, a friend, a partner, an adviser—lawyer, banker, life insurance man, accountant. But distinguish clearly between the other person's role as a sounding board and as a true adviser. The sounding-board function helps you make up your mind about your beneficiaries and what they need; your assets and their value to your family; the proper balance between providing for your own future and your family's future; and the directions and the objectives of your estate planning. But the advisory role is equally important—to delineate the alternatives available to you; to explain how you and your family can be protected yet not be put in a strait jacket; and to spell out the various ways that present spending ability and future flexibility can be balanced against present and future tax savings and protection before and after your death.

Then, you must make the decisions, and your lawyer must undertake the responsibility of implementing those decisions.

What are the steps? This book will take you through them in this way:

1. First consider the people you want to provide for. You must think about what they need; their faults and capabilities; what opportunities they should have and can handle; what burdens they should be spared; and what possible weaknesses they should be protected against. What protective devices are available to you?

2. Review your assets. The assets establish the basic character of the estate. An estate usually falls into one or a combination of four patterns:

(a) a bundle of inherited or created capital (securities, real estate, etc.);

(b) a family business;

(c) a bundle of payroll rights (options, contracts, pension or profit-sharing rights, group insurance); or

(d) painfully accumulated savings supplemented by insurance policies.

Almost any significant estate will fall into one or a combination of these patterns. You have to take a hard look at each asset. What do they do for you and your family now? What are they likely to do in the future? How much security and freedom do they represent for you now—for your family later on? What is it worth in each of these four ways:

(a) How much income and satisfaction are they producing now?

(b) What price would they bring now and how much of it would you keep?

(c) How would they be valued for estate tax purposes?

(d) How much cash would your executor be able to realize from them?

3. What is the best way to transfer these assets to your family? There are twelve broad ways to transfer your property, and they have different costs and different effects during your life and after your death. Reviewing these will point up the alternatives available to you.

4. What will your estate do for your family as it stands? What will the tax collector want? Where would the necessary cash come from? What would be left? This is mostly mathematics, but it will be very revealing and helpful in shaping up what you will want to do.

5. How can you cut down the liabilities of your estate and the amount of cash your executor will need? There are only two major ways to accomplish this: transfer assets out of your estate now; take advantage of tax exemptions (primarily the marital deduction, which exempts a portion of your estate transferred to your spouse).

6. How can you increase the estate and raise the necessary cash? Apart from making some kind of killing, which most people don't do and which is always unpredictable, there are only two ways—buy life insurance and arrange for the most

efficient accumulation of income (this is part investment, part tax planning).

7. How can you set up assets for your family now? Here you should consider gifts, living trusts, insurance and annuity arrangements, and joint ownership.

8. What is the best way for your assets to be transferred at death? Here you consider probate and its avoidance; what your will should cover and what it should say; trusts set up now and after your death; whether in trusts created now you should emphasize tax savings, by giving up the right to change your mind, or flexibility, by reserving the power to take the property back.

9. Is there enough, and do you want to do something for charity? Can you benefit yourself and your family by doing something for charity?

10. Select the people you are going to rely on to help you construct and carry out your plan. Get financial advice about your assets and income and its potentials from a life underwriter, your banker, and your accountant. However, in the final construction and implementation of your plan, you must rely on a competent lawyer. In picking one, look for knowledge and understanding of your affairs, experience with proven responsibility, and an outlook that emphasizes flexibility, protection from legal pitfalls, and maximum tax savings. Finally, and possibly most important, pick an experienced, responsible executor and trustee who is certain to have the time and the resources of knowledge and organization that your affairs will require.

CHAPTER II

HOW TO THINK ABOUT
YOUR BENEFICIARIES

Ask yourself these questions about each member of your family:

(1) What will his financial position be?

(2) What will he need?

(3) What is his capacity?

(4) Should he get capital—and when?

(5) Can he manage money?

(6) Should he be protected from administrative and investment responsibilities and burdens?

(7) What kind of assets—education, capital, business interest—may he need to best develop his life and to take care of his family?

(8) Does he have any special legal rights? Or liabilities? Or disabilities?

(9) Are any special arrangements—trust funds, cash bequests, withdrawal rights, guardians, waivers—indicated to deal with these rights, liabilities, or disabilities?

YOUR WIFE AS BENEFICIARY

Your wife is ordinarily not only the prime beneficiary of the estate, but also the prime asset of the family. Her death before that of the husband will not only deprive the family of the guidance and services she provides but may also increase its annual income-tax cost and sharply increase the cash needed to meet the cost of the husband's death. This asset status of a wife may call for insurance on her life to

7

cover the increased cash liabilities that would result from her death.

Most states require that a specified portion of a man's estate be granted to his wife, and she is given the power to elect this share against her husband's will. The share ranges from a life interest in one-third of the husband's real estate to half his entire estate outright. It varies from state to state and sometimes within a given state, depending on the number of children who survive the husband. In some states the wife can waive these rights. In others, she can't. Usually these rights do not apply against insurance proceeds. Sometimes the widow's rights cannot be asserted against property tranferred to the children or to trusts by the husband during his life.

A divorce, after making a will, may automatically revoke all provisions in favor of and relating to the divorced spouse. A marriage after making a will may give a surviving spouse a right to the intestate share (what the law gives if there is no will) in addition to the right "to take against the will," that is, to take the share the law gives her. These provisions may vary from state to state.

Property bequeathed to your wife outright or in a trust qualifying for the so-called marital deduction will be exempt from federal estate tax on your death to the extent of 50 per cent of your adjusted gross estate. You must pass up this tax saving if you want to control who is to get your property when your wife dies. Property in excess of the marital deduction bequeathed to your wife is exposed to a second estate tax on your wife's subsequent death. For this reason, it may be desirable to place property to remain available for the use of your wife, to the extent that it exceeds the marital deduction, in a trust. Then, it will be taxed only on your death and not a second time when your wife dies. Your wife's security can be protected by giving her income rights in this trust.

If, for income-tax saving purposes, you find it desirable to accumulate the income or distribute it directly to children, your wife can be given access to the principal of either the marital deduction trust, the children's trust, or both. No limit is required on her access to the marital deduction portion for tax reasons because that will be taxed in her estate in any event. But to save estate taxes on her death, her access to the capital of the second trust should be limited to the trustee's discretion, based on maintaining living standards and emergency needs, or if on her demand, to the extent of $5,000 a year or 5 per cent of the trust corpus, whichever is higher.

In making provisions for a wife, these are the usual guide lines:

(1) Give her all the income for her life, unless the estate is so large that she will clearly not need it all and it will result in excessive income tax costs.

(2) In a two-trust plan, it may be best to give her all the income from one trust plus the right to consume capital from that trust and to have income distributed directly to children or accumulated in the other trust. This will reduce the amount of the estate that will be taxed on the wife's death. She can be protected against a falling off of income either by giving her withdrawal rights or by giving the trustee discretion to distribute principal from the second trust.

(3) Whenever there is a possibility that the income from the estate will be insufficient to maintain the wife adequately, give her the limited right to withdraw capital and, in addition, give the trustees discretion to make additional distributions to her from capital when necessary to maintain her living standards and to meet illness or other emergency costs.

(4) On the wife's death, the capital tied up in trust to support her can then be made available to children. Here we have the consideration as to how much to make available for

the children and when. The person making a will must also consider whether or not to set up a rigid distribution pattern in his will or merely to give his wife a so-called power of appointment so that she can decide how the capital is to be distributed, depending on the circumstances, the financial condition, and the needs of the children at some time subsequent to the husband's death when she makes her last will.

Decide whether and to what extent capital should be given outright to the wife. The considerations here are (1) the value of relieving her of administrative and investment burdens, (2) protecting her from the burden of demands from others, and (3) protecting her and the children from indiscretion and folly in investing or otherwise disposing of funds.

CHILDREN AS BENEFICIARIES

The trick here is to measure needs and interests in life as well as weaknesses and capabilities and then to design provisions to match them. The property owner must formulate his philosophy as to when children should come into possession of money and whether they should have access to the capital or merely use of the income. If there is small capital, they usually get it outright at some appropriate age. If there is large capital, it may be considered that the income will be enough for them, that a portion of the capital will be enough for them, or that they should get all the capital but not all at once but in two or three payments separated by five to ten years in time. If they are going to dissipate your money, this gives them a chance to learn from their mistakes and, at least, prevents them from squandering it all at once.

Where capital is tied up, it is important that a mechanism be established so that children will be able to get sums large enough to meet educational requirements and perhaps set up a home or get started in business. This can be done readily by appropriate capital invasion provisions, either in the discretion of the trustee or on call of the children. There are no serious adverse tax consequences as to the latter, provided a single year's invasion is limited to 5 per cent of the corpus or $5,000, whichever is higher.

Unless the estate is fairly large, the usual thing is to provide no benefits for the children until the wife dies. Where there is a large estate, it may be desirable to make gifts to the children during life and to set up trusts for them under the father's will. Whether the children are provided for by gift, by bequests or trusts created directly for them under the will, or by distributions from a trust created for their mother after her death, we face the problem of when to make the funds available to the children. A decision is necessary as to whether it is healthy and wholesome to permit the children to come into substantial funds at age 21. Is it better to have the funds conserved until they have attained more experience and a mature age? Should all the funds be made available to them at once? Perhaps it is safer to give them the funds in two or three installments. Safer still, if the estate is large enough, enough capital to produce eating money may be kept in trust for life.

Some parents want to have the child's share held in trust for life so that they can control who gets the property after the child's death and in order to save estate taxes on his death. It is doubtful whether either of these reasons is good enough to keep property tied up in trust for a child's life so that the child will never be able to use anything but the income from the property.

It will be necessary to decide whether all children are to be treated alike. The fact is, of course, that children are not alike. They vary in stability, judgment, competence, sex, physical make-up, and so on. A parent usually spends funds in accordance with the needs of the children, making no attempt to equalize the amount spent for education, medical care, ond so on. By postponing a division of the estate into separate shares until the youngest living child reaches a designated age and by directing that until that time, income and principal shall be used for the benefit of the children in accordance with their needs in amounts not necessarily equal, the practical situation can remain the same after the parent's death as before. This plan is particularly sensible where the estate is modest and the children are young. Another way to accomplish substantially this result is to permit the estate to be divided into separate shares but to direct that specified expenditures for any one child, such as medical and educational expenses be charged equally against all shares rather than against the share of the particular child benefited by the expenditures.

There are other problems with children arising from the special protection the law gives them and from the many different kinds of children that can exist—grandchildren and stepchildren and adopted children and illegitimate children and posthumous children. A posthumous child, one born after the death of a parent, generally inherits along with the other children under a broad provision in a will or where there is no will.

In most states, the law provides that when a child is born after the will is executed, the child is entitled to the share the law would give him if there were no will. In certain states, the case of an after-born child may result in the revocation of a will.

Most states recognize that adopted children have the same rights as children born of the marriage in the matter of wills and descent of property. However, the protection given to children by the law regarding wills is not always accorded in life insurance beneficiary arrangements. If a father neglects to change his life insurance beneficiary arrangements after a child is born, or if he dies while his wife is pregnant, the child may not receive any proceeds. Similarly, unless an adopted child is specifically named as the beneficiary, he will not receive any insurance proceeds.

In most states, illegitimate children inherit from their mother but not from their father unless their parenthood is formally recognized. Again, this protection does not follow over into life insurance.

You must be careful to see that will or insurance provisions for children cover after-born children by providing for children as a class or by specifiying that children born later are to be covered as well as those in being when you execute your will or name insurance beneficiaries. It is similarly important to specify whether or not adopted children are to be treated as natural children. Although state law frequently makes such provision for after-born children and creates a presumption for adopted children, it is better to cover the status of these children expressly. You may move to another state.

THE INCOMPETENT, CHILD

The problem in providing for an incompetent child is one of custody and adequate financial provision for life. This overriding requirement may call for all the capital the parents have been able to amass. There may not be enough capital to provide lifetime assurance, and this may suggest the possibility of public institutional care at some point. This may call for a change of residence so that the parent can assure himself that the most satisfactory public institution will be available to the child if that should be ultimately necessary.

Where there are enough funds, a trust should be created to provide maintenance, including institutional care. The important thing is to provide independent financial support for the incompetent or *possibly* incompetent child, not only to assure the child's security but to remove the burden from his brothers and sisters. This is in the interest of the incompetent child as well as that of the brothers and sisters. Here it is especially important that a guardian or committee be appointed to control the incompetent's money.

GRANDCHILDREN AS BENEFICIARIES

In the main, the problems of income provision and capital distribution are the same for grandchildren as for children. However, there is the frequently overlooked problem of how best to spread out the family wealth among grandchildren after their parents, the grandparent's children, die. The usual provision is that on the death of children, property held in trust for them should be distributed "per stirpes." This provision divides the property into as many equal parts as there are children living or children dead with issue living, with one part passing to each living child and one part passing to the children, collectively, of each deceased child.

A so-called per stirpes distribution treats each branch of the family equally, but people live as individuals, not as branches of a family.

It may be more equitable to provide a so-called "per capita" distribution. This gives an equal amount to each individual grandchild. Here is an example of how these two forms of distribution work. If you had two children, both of whom die before you, one having only one child and the other having five, a per stirpes distribution will make one of the six grandchildren five times richer than the other five. A per capita distribution would give them all equal wealth. The problem of after-born grandchildren, as well as the problem of some children living much longer than others and thus keeping property put in trust for them tied up that much longer, makes a per capita distribution very complicated to work out. This may account for the greater popularity of the per stirpes distribution. However, careful draftsmanship can work out satisfactory per capita arrangements.

GUARDIANSHIP

When property is left to a child, he can't get the property himself. Neither the bank holding the parent's account nor the corporation that has issued stock owned by either parent nor the executor or administrator of the parent's estate can make payment to a child. Transfer of the property to a person under 21 may be made to him only if a guardian is appointed by the court for his benefit. Unless husband and wife select a guardian to take their place in the event that both should die, the court will have to appoint one without their help.

Guardianship has two aspects: (1) Who is to have personal control of the minor? (2) Who is to manage the minor's property? Both functions may be carried out by the same person, or a separate guardian of the person and guardian of the property may be appointed. Neither parent can appoint a guardian of the person of the child other than the surviving spouse, unless the survivor is incompetent or otherwise clearly incapable or unfit. But the first spouse to die, like any other person, can appoint anyone as guardian of the property he leaves to the child. The surviving spouse will generally have the right to designate in her or his will a guardian both of the property and of the person of the child.

If the parents make no such appointment, or if they both

appoint different persons and they die at the same time in a common disaster, the probate court will make the appointment. The child becomes a ward of the court, and the court must determine which appointment will best serve the welfare of the child and then select a guardian accordingly. The next of kin will ordinarily be given preference but not necessarily so. Frequently, the same person will be appointed both guardian of the person and of the property but sometimes a separation of these functions is justified. For example, an aunt of the child might clearly be the right choice to be guardian of the person, but she may be so inexperienced in investment and finances that another person will be appointed guardian of the property.

The important thing is that the selection of the guardian is a matter that should be given careful attention. It is frequently overlooked entirely; probably the assumption is that the surviving spouse will perform the function. This is correct as far as it goes, but it fails when both parents die in a common disaster and when a surviving spouse fails to consider the problem and to designate the guardian in his or her will. Not only should the selection of the guardian be given careful thought before the selection is made, but the matter should be discussed with the prospective guardian. Also, an alternate or successor guardian should be named in case the first one is dead or declines to act or he undertakes the responsibility and later wants to resign or is unable to complete the work.

The rules concerning guardianship vary from state to state. The handling of property by a guardian is always a cumbersome, expensive process. Unless the will exempts an individual named as guardian, he will be required to provide bond either by putting up his own property or buying a surety bond, the cost of which will be a charge against the infant's property. A bank is not usually required to post a bond, but most banks are unwilling to act as guardian of the person. The guardian must meet the expense of periodic accountings out of the child's property.

The consent of the court is usually required before any of the child's money is spent. If the child's parent is the guardian, the court will not permit the use of any of the child's funds if the parent has the means to support the child. However, if a widowed mother is a guardian and has insufficient means of her own, a court may permit use of the child's property to enable the mother to maintain a home for the child.

Sometimes an uncle or aunt is expected to take care of a child after the death of the parents, but no thought is given to the financial burden that it will represent. It may mean a larger house. It will almost certainly mean expenses over and above those the court will allow the guardian to make on behalf of the child. This is something that should be faced, discussed, and where possible, covered with an adequate financial provision of some kind for the probable guardian.

There is one way to avoid all the red tape that goes with guardianship. The will can authorize either an executor or a trustee to hold a child's property and to administer it as though he were guardian. The best way is to put the property in trust for the child and to give the trustee the right to pay over the income and a portion of the principal when needed for support, either directly to the child, to his personal guardian, to the person with whom he lives, or to others for the child's benefit. The trustee can then be given the power to accumulate any balance not needed for the child's care. The trustee should be given this power not only concerning trust funds set up primarily for the child, but also concerning any portion of a trust fund that by virtue of the death of prior beneficiaries or otherwise, is distributable to the child.

PARENTS OR OTHER ELDER
MEMBERS OF THE FAMILY

Frequently a property owner will have been making regular contributions to (or otherwise supporting) his parents or uncle or aunts or older brothers or sisters. He will usually want to continue this support after his death. This can be done by an outright bequest of cash, by having the will provide income payments, or by setting up a trust to last for the beneficiary's life, with the trust property then reverting to the property owner's wife or children or a limited-period trust set up for them. Or, if there are trusts set up by the will, it can be directed that these trusts pay out the required income. It is sometimes desirable to direct or authorize the executor to buy an annuity to continue payments to a relative. In some instances, this can avoid tying up the estate for the rest of the relative's life.

The least expensive way of providing for elderly relatives may be a so-called short-term, or reverter, trust, which is discussed in Chapter XIII.

THE FORGOTTEN WOMAN

The late Surrogate Foley of New York applied this term to daughters-in-law. Sons-in-law are much less of a problem; usually they can take care of themselves. But sometimes there is a lot of money from the mother's side that has accustomed the children to a living standard that the son-in-law can't keep up if his wife should die, unless some of her family money is placed in trust for the grandchildren.

The acute problem is with the daughter-in-law. Typically, the grandfather will provide that the father will have the income from the trust for life, and upon his death, the principal is to go to his children. The daughter-in-law is completely bypassed. When her husband dies, she must rely on her children for support. If they are not of legal age, she must act under cumbersome red tape and expensive bond as their guardian and go into court to obtain annual decrees permitting her to make modest use of the children's funds for their maintenance and for her own. Then when the children come of age she is no longer entitled to any relief from the court and becomes wholly dependent on her children and on her own earning capacity.

The best way to deal with this problem is to give the son a so-called power of appointment over a portion of the trust. This will permit him to make appropriate provisions for his wife. If you do this, make sure that he knows about the existence of the power of appointment and prod him into making proper use of it. The grandfather can provide for maintenance of his daughter-in-law while her family is growing up when he provides for his son and grandchildren in his own will. The important thing is to provide something for the daughter-in-law after the grandchildren, her own children, have attained their majorities. She may have held back on remarrying in order to devote herself to her children, and she should be protected from being entirely dependent on them when they have grown up.

CHAPTER III

HOW TO THINK ABOUT YOUR PROPERTY

Ask yourself these questions about each of your assets:

1. What value would be placed on it for estate tax purposes? You need this to determine the cash liabilities that your estate will face and how much cash has to be raised and what will be left for your family after all the cash liabilities have been satisfied.

2. What does this asset do for my personal, business, investment, and retirement needs?

3. Does this asset need my experience and skill to maintain its value?

4. What is the liquidity value of this asset? How much would its real value be discounted if it were necessary to dispose of it quickly in order to raise cash for my estate or its beneficiaries?

5. What would this asset do for my family? How much annual income will it produce? Should it be switched into other income-producing assets? What would the capital gains tax on such a switch be now and after my death keeping in mind the availability of a stepped-up basis on death?

Only after you have looked at each asset in this way will you be in a position to appreciate the magnitude of the cash liabilities your estate will face, the difficulty of raising the necessary cash, and the ability of your estate to support your family without your earning capacity. This will force you to consider whether each of your assets is worth retaining now and at the time of your death and to lay the basis for a review of your investment policy as well as your estate arrangements.

YOUR PERSONAL PROPERTY

As you know, almost all types of property except land, buildings, and things attached to either are personal property. If personal property that might be included in your taxable estate really belongs to someone else, steps should be taken to make the real ownership clear. In some states, there is a presumption that furniture in a house owned or rented by the husband belongs to him. If, in fact, it belongs to the wife, recitations in the will and a record showing the true ownership should be enough to make its ownership clear (evidence of gifts from the wife's family, bills or checks showing payment by the wife, etc.). This will keep that much value out of your taxable estate.

Personal possessions like books and paintings may carry a value that will produce tax liability out of all proportion to their value and interest to your family or to what the estate can afford to pay to keep them. This dilemma may be avoided by having this kind of property go to an existing museum or charity or one created for the family by the will itself.

BANK ACCOUNTS AND SECURITIES

Make up a list of securities owned and check to see that they are registered properly in order to avoid confusion after death. Make sure that securities or a bank account held in any fiduciary or agency capacity are clearly indicated and that the real interest of the parties involved is stated in writing. Have the securities kept in one place, preferably in the state of domicile, that is, where you have your permanent residence. This will avoid possible double taxation and requirements of administration in more than one state. For the same reason, it is desirable to maintain all bank accounts in the state of domicile.

In reviewing your security portfolio, consider eliminating those that may present troublesome valuation problems. If there are any notes of children or other members of the family, determine whether they are to be forgiven, collected, or set off against a legacy.

ASSETS LOCATED IN ANOTHER STATE OR ANOTHER COUNTRY

Consider what can be done to avoid the cost of ancillary administration. When you reside in one state and have assets in another state or country, there is always a chance that your personal representatives may have to go into the courts of the state or country where the assets are located to establish their claim to them. If this is needed, it is known as ancillary administration. One way to avoid this is to transfer the property to a life trust now; another is to transfer it to a family corporation. You have to determine who can qualify as ancillary executor or ancillary administrator in the other state or foreign country. It will also be necessary to find out about the requirements concerning the disposition of property by will or otherwise, the administering of the property, and any death or other taxes. Unless the will is executed according to the law of the other state or country, property located there may be treated in the same way as though you didn't have a will, and it would pass according to the foreign laws.

MUTUAL FUNDS

The same considerations applying to securities generally apply to mutual funds and other investment company holdings. Some extra thought must go into planning for the disposition of these assets, however, if they are to be used as the principal or a part of the principal of a trust set up in your will or if there may be a prolonged delay before the estate assets are finally distributed to beneficiaries. If you already own mutual funds and wish them partially or fully to fund a will-created trust, make sure that your will provides in no uncertain terms that your executor and trustee are empowered to retain such shares and to invest further in such shares, notwithstanding any possible state statute or case law holding that such retention or purchase was not permitted. Otherwise, depending on local law, it might be necessary to sell the mutual fund shares, and it might be impossible for the trustee to reinvest in these types of shares.

The question of allocation of mutual fund capital gains distributions between income and corpus of the trust should also be resolved by an appropriate provision in the will. If this is not done, local law will determine how these distributions are to be allocated.

In a given estate, it may prove necessary for your executor to withhold distributions for a relatively long time. And in the absence of a specific authorization to the executor to retain so-called nonlegal investments, in a number of states the executor will be required to dispose of the mutual fund shares. It is therefore advisable that your will contain a clause specifically empowering your executor to retain and even to reinvest distributions (if this is desired) in mutual fund shares.

OIL AND GAS INTERESTS

Usually, an oil interest turns out to be some sort of realty interest, and quite often it is located in a state other than where the estate owner lives. Oil and gas interests (leasehold interests, royalty interests, working interests, production payments, net-profit interests, etc.) can be very difficult assets to administer in the estate, and sometimes it is preferable to arrange for their disposition prior to or shortly after death. Where these interests are to be retained for beneficiaries, many estate planners urge that they be given to beneficiaries via bequests and devises rather than as part of the general or trust estate. They reason that leaving such interests in the general or trust estate sometimes places too serious an investment burden on the shoulders of the fiduciary. And, unless to do so might bar him from further participation in a venture, he may very well prefer to sit on his hands rather than commit further monies to the oil or gas venture.

Where, despite the above admonitions, for one reason or another oil and gas interests are to form a part of your general or trust estate, it will be necessary to give your executor or trustee, as the case may be, a substantial array of special powers:

1. This is a highly complex investment area; the fiduciary must be given the authority to rely on the advice of experts without incurring any personal liability for acting on this advice and, if necessary, to pay for this advice.

2. Where a fiduciary is to be given the power to retain oil and gas interests, you must decide whether you want them retained even if the interest is unproductive. And if the answer is yes, then a provision to that effect belongs in the will.

3. Any authority to invest or reinvest in additional oil and gas ventures should specifically refer to the type of interest (leasehold, royalty, working, etc.) you have in mind or should be sufficiently broad to include any of these if this is your intention.

4. In a working interest, it is a good idea to give your fiduciary power to participate in any reorganization and to invest any additional monies as may be necessary for the

further exploration, development, and preservation of such interest.

5. It is also a good idea to give your fiduciary specific leasing powers, as well as the power to drill, test, and explore for further minerals.

6. It is very important that the fiduciary be given broad authority to allocate income and expenses of oil and gas interests without regard to local law and to establish such depletion reserves as it deems desirable.

REAL ESTATE

Your family home can be both an asset and a liability. It may cost more to run than your family can afford out of the income from your estate.

If the family is to continue to live in the family residence after your death, it is best to leave it outright to your widow or to the children if they are of age. It is important to determine how state law treats any mortgage on the real estate and to make it clear in your will whether the real estate is given free and clear of the mortgage and whether or not your executor is to leave the mortgage outstanding or to pay it off.

If you have real estate other than the home, it is important that the estate not be burdened with carrying it along if it is unproductive. You should either authorize or direct the sale of real estate that is not producing an income for the beneficiary.

REAL ESTATE SYNDICATE INTERESTS

If you are a participant in one or more real estate syndicates (usually of the limited partnership variety), special provisions should be inserted in your will.

(1) Your executor should be authorized to comply with all the terms and provisions of the syndicate agreement and to execute and deliver to the general partners the requisite designation of a successor to your interest. (A similar authorization should be given to any trustee except for the designation of a successor.)

(2) Fiduciaries should be empowered to vote and exercise all rights and also to execute all required consents in regard to such property, just as if they were the absolute owners.

(3) If such property is not specifically bequeathed, then it might be a good idea to authorize the executor to make distributions in kind.

(4) Where an interest in a real estate syndication is to be used as all or part of the principal of trust, the trustees can be directed to allocate all distributions to income, if this is your desire, regardless of the fact that a portion of such distributions may be a return of capital for accounting and tax purposes. Also to be considered is the question of whether or not to treat mortgage amortization payments as income.

FARMS

If you own a working farm, it will have the attributes of real estate and of a business. In transferring a farm by will or deed of trust, the person who drafts your will or deed must deal with land, buildings, machinery, equipment, livestock, accounts receivable, bank accounts, insurance policies, crops, real estate mortgages, and so on. If the farm is incorporated, all these assets are reflected by the shares of stock, and the problem is greatly simplified. In addition, there may be income-tax savings and capital-building opportunities in the incorporation of the farm.

When you give farmland by will you must decide whether

the person who gets it is to be exonerated for mortgage debt from the balance of your estate. In some states, unless he is explicitly made responsible for the mortgage debt, this will occur. In any event, the burden of the mortgage debt should be explicitly fixed. Also specify whether debts incurred in connection with the improvement of buildings or the purchase of equipment are to be assumed by him or paid out of the general estate. If you don't, there may be some uncertainty as to the intended result and unnecessary conflicts may arise.

Insurance policies covering farm buildings and equipment should be specifically included in the gift of the farm. Livestock, machinery, stored crops, and other farm personal property should also be specifically included. State the rights to growing crops, if there is any doubt. Specify whether the beneficiary gets the accounts receivable owing by virtue of produce or livestock sold and, if so, specify how uncollectible accounts are to be treated.

It is necessary to give the executor or trustee authority to carry on the farm operation alone, as a partner or shareholder; to hire labor and managers or get tenants; to buy and sell machinery, equipment or livestock; to reconstruct, repair, and improve farm buildings; to borrow money; to carry on operations or to make improvements; to sell all or part of the farm business; to subdivide or otherwise convert the farm property to new uses; to retain income from working capital and to set up reserves out of income for cattle purchases, building improvements, fences, tilling, fertilizer, etc. Perhaps the trustee should also be authorized to incorporate the farm business, to sell it to your children on special terms or options, to lease it to members of the family, to build new buildings, to continue and improve herds, or to mortgage the farm to provide funds for beneficiaries.

LIFE INSURANCE POLICIES

These fall into two categories—those on your own life and those on someone else's life. The face value of those on your own life can be taken out of the estate tax by transferring the policies to the beneficiaries. Policies you own on someone else's life should probably not go to that person on your death. If they do, the cash value will be taxed on your death, and the face value will be taxed on the death of the person insured. Your will should probably direct that these policies go to the beneficiaries of the insured or to a trust for their benefit. If they go into trust, the will should give proper discretion as to payment of premiums maturing between the death of the owner and that of the insured. Should the policy be transferred by bequest or sale to the insured, or should it be cashed in or converted to paid-up insurance, or should it be carried as an investment, and in that event, where will the premium money come from?

Study the policies themselves and the beneficiary designations. Go over these questions with your insurance adviser:

(1) What ages do the policies show? If there are different ages, get proof of age and make the appropriate corrections.

(2) Who are the beneficiaries?

(3) Who are the contingent beneficiaries? Are new marriages and new births reflected?

(4) What settlement options have been elected? Have they been left optional or made automatic?

(5) Are proceeds protected from claims of creditors?

(6) Are proceeds judgment-proof to beneficiaries?

(7) Will the proceeds qualify for the marital deduction?

(8) Is there an automatic loan provision to make the policies lapse-proof?

(9) Is there a waiver of premium on disability?

(10) Is there an accidental death benefit? Would it be preferable to take an additional term rider to provide added benefits if death is from sickness instead of accident?

(11) Can worthwhile savings be made by shifting premium payments to annual basis, by discounting future premiums?

(12) Are dividends on participating policies being used to best advantage—to buy additions, to maintain amount of risk account over increasing cash value?

(13) Are there any loans? If loans have been paid up, have assignments of policies been released? Should loans be refinanced? Is it clear whether loans will be payable out of proceeds only, or is residual estate also liable?

(14) If owner is other than insured and beneficiary is a different person, has the gift tax risk been considered?

(15) Are simultaneous death and short-time survivorship contingencies accurately provided for? Do they furnish maximum protection for marital deduction or against diversion of proceeds and double administration?

(16) What savings can be had by change of ownership?

(17) What savings or added flexibility can be achieved by change of beneficiaries?

BUSINESS INTERESTS

If you own all or part of a business, you face a multitude of especially difficult problems. The real value of the business may depend on your skill and energy. The business usually represents a large percentage of the total estate that is not liquid, unless special arrangements are made to convert it into cash. And the value of this nonliquid asset is likely to create a large cash tax liability. Unless funds are made available to meet this liability, disastrous results may follow.

You will have to decide whether the business should be held by your family or sold in order to buy investment quality producing assets. You will have to consider the desirability of a buy-sell arrangement with your business associates. You will have to consider how you can get cash out of your business. Ask yourself these questions about the business:

(1) Is it purely personal service; does it depend entirely on your personal talent or following? If so, can it be turned over to other ownership with advantage to your family, customers, or employees?

(2) Does it have going concern value in the form of tangible assets, reputation, trade position, location, knowhow, or other factors independent of you? Is it large enough to support a second tier of management that can be trained to carry on?

(3) Does your family have potential capacity for ownership and management?

(4) If not, is the business substantial enough to support hired management?

(5) Is your family capable of supervision?

(6) Can other arrangements be made for adequate ownership supervision of hired management?

(7) Does your family have a financial cushion so that its security is not entirely dependent on a business under new management?

(8) Are the risks of continued family ownership justified by the promise of a much greater investment return or the desire to hold the business as a vehicle for maturing children?

(9) Can assets be withdrawn or additional funds created to hedge this risk?

(10) How much of a cushion can be created by using some of the business income to carry insurance on your life?

(11) Is the business profitable enough to justify its continuance? What are its future prospects?

If the decision is to sell, the job is to find a market that will provide a good price for the business. If the decision is to retain, there are various degrees of retention. It may be sufficient to retain working control. The need to raise cash to pay death taxes on the value of the business and the desirability of providing a stake for successor management are factors that push in the direction of retaining only control rather than 100 per cent ownership.

Then you will have to decide among the following main alternatives:

(1) Sell the business to outsiders during life, when you may be able to work out the best deal.

(2) Get liquidity by selling part of the business to the public and starting a market in the stock.

(3) Enter into a buy-and-sell arrangement with co-stockholders and fund it so as to establish a market at death.

(4) Sell or give part of the business to others in the family, employees, or both—and work out a stock redemption plan that will give the estate cash out of the business.

(5) Recapitalize to reduce the value of control stock and proceed as in (4) above.

(6) Let the business pass by will and direct your executor to get enough cash out of it to pay death costs and provide for your widow.

No matter what the plan, these two steps are essential.

(1) Have your will explicitly give to your executor all authority necessary to retain the stock and to operate the business.

(2) See that there is insurance or some other definite source of liquid funds to meet the obligations that mature at death.

THE PAYROLL ESTATE

These days, most people acquire most of their capital through pension and profit-sharing plans, stock options, group insurance, and other fringe benefits that their corporate employer makes available. If you are like most people, special problems facing you in this kind of an estate include the following:

1. Your company has promised you a major build-up in capital value—provided you stay alive and continue to function satisfactorily for the company. If you die before the company's promises are fulfilled, your family will lose this projected capital value.

2. A substantial part of your estate is likely to be in death benefits or equities in a qualified pension, profit-sharing, stock-bonus, or savings plan, which if properly handled can be transferred free of estate tax.

3. Insurance benefits are likely to make up a large part of your estate, and it may be possible to have these values transferred free of estate tax. You must also be alert to the possibility that maturing insurance values may be needed to pay estate tax that falls due on other nonliquid assets or to conserve the values available to your estate in unexercised stock options.

4. A large part of the taxable value of your estate may consist of rights to future income, to be realized by the estate and its beneficiaries only over a period of time. This may create a liquidity problem.

5. A large part of the potential value of the estate may consist of stock options. If these are still unexercised at death, your executor will usually have to exercise them within a specified and limited number of months after death in order to conserve the value of any latent and unrealized appreciation in the stock to which the options apply.

6. A substantial part of the value of your estate may consist of rights to receive future income that, after the first $5,000, will be subject to income tax on receipt. If these rights to deferred compensation go to your widow, they will be subject after two years to income tax without benefit of splitting on joint return, unless she remarries. This may bring high income-tax rates into play even though your salary no longer swells the family income. These income rights can be more effectively converted to permanent capital for the family if your will directs that they be distributed to a number of taxable entities such as your wife, your children directly, or trusts for the wife and children.

7. Your ability to accumulate capital outside of the corporation will be impaired by the fact that investment income will be received by you on top of high earned income and thus fall subject to high income-tax rates. This suggests the desirability of transferring investment assets to a reversionary trust or, if you can afford to part with the capital, to an accumulating trust for your wife and children, or directly to your children, if this can be done under the state law.

8. You may not be able to take advantage of one of the most effective estate tax saving techniques, that of making lifetime gifts, because most of your assets will somehow be tied in with your corporate employment so that it will not be practicable to make them the subject of a lifetime gift. If you are in that position, it may make sense for you to borrow in order to acquire assets that can be given directly to your family. The assets given to your family can thus be made free of estate tax, and your borrowing will reduce your taxable estate. Needless to say, this approach must be used with great caution in order to avoid impairing your personal security and peace of mind.

WHAT TO DO ABOUT PAYROLL ASSETS IN YOUR ESTATE

Pension and Profit-Sharing Interests: The plan will ordinarily provide a mechanism for designating the beneficiary to receive the amount accumulated when you die. By naming individual beneficiaries rather than your estate, you can avoid estate tax on the amount accumulated from the employer's contribution. By naming a trust for your family as beneficiary, you can save estate tax at the death of your wife and other beneficiaries of the family trust.

Study the plan itself. What elections does it make available? Consider the income-tax liability when the accumulated benefits are received; see that the successor beneficiaries are named.

Amounts accumulated in a pension or profit-sharing plan from the employer's contribution pass free of estate tax if made payable to a named beneficiary. They are subject to estate tax if payable to your estate. Estate tax can be skipped for the lives of both you and your wife (children too) if benefits are made payable to a trust that suspends distribution.

Stock Options: Study the plan and the option contract. How much time is allowed to exercise the options after death? Will any income-tax liability accrue at death? Has your executor been specifically authorized to exercise the options and to borrow money or sell assets quickly for that purpose? Should insurance be provided to facilitate the exercise of options?

Deferred Compensation Contracts: Are any benefits available to your family? What can be done to minimize income-tax liability? Should your executor be directed as to how to distribute these rights?

HOW TO HANDLE YOUR
GROUP LIFE INSURANCE PROCEEDS

Group life insurance, generally, is the coverage of a number of employees under a master or single life insurance policy, which enables the employer to provide insurance coverage on the life of his employees at a cost below what it would normally cost these employees if they were to purchase such coverage on an individual basis. The employees are insured for a flat premium, which is based on the average age of the "group" (participants). Generally, these premiums are paid by the employer (noncontributory plan), but a portion of the premium may also be paid by the employee if desired (contributory plan).

By designating someone other than your estate as beneficiary, you can keep the group insurance proceeds out of your probate estate and escape state inheritance taxes. But you have a problem escaping federal estate taxes.

Until now, it has been quite difficult, if not impossible, to work out an assignment of the "incidents of ownership" with a group insurance policy. For one thing, the policies themselves quite often are made nonassignable on their face. And even where this was not the case or where the insurance company was willing to waive the nonassignability provision, state law often creeps into the picture to apparently nullify an assignment.

In any event, the Treasury has unofficially taken the position that group insurance assignments are ineffective—and that the proceeds, notwithstanding the attempted assignment, are still to be included in the employee-insured's estate. This is because the Treasury feels that an employee does not have sufficient ownership in his group insurance contract to be able to give away his interest.

A number of companies, while being careful not to advise

employees about the possible tax results of group insurance policy assignments, are nevertheless notifying their employees that their insurance carriers are willing to effectuate policy assignments. Major corporations have sent out notices to all their employees covered under their insurance plan that arrangements had been worked out with the insurance carrier to permit any employee who so requests to file an irrevocable assignment of his life insurance and accidental death coverage.

By making such a transfer, while there is no guarantee, there is a possibility that the proceeds will escape taxes. If you do nothing, the proceeds are certain to be included in your estate. You lose nothing by making the transfer; you only gain a possible tax savings.

CHAPTER IV

TWELVE WAYS TO
TRANSFER YOUR PROPERTY

The transfer of property to the next generation is at best an expensive procedure. If you do nothing at all, it will be done for you by the probate procedure; that is, the procedure set up by law that the courts carry out. And that may be the worst way to have it done.

Here we help you to evaluate the several alternatives available and to select the method best for your family.

Whether you have your property probated or use one of the other methods of property transfer can be an important decision to you. But it is far from the most important choice you can make in arranging your property so that it will do what you want it to do for your family. This book will suggest how you should think about your property and your income and how you can arrange it to achieve the independence you want for yourself and your family.

The probate procedure will designate someone to act as your personal representative. If you leave a will, the person named as your executor or personal representative will be named. If you fail to leave a will, the probate court—known variously in the different states as probate, surrogate, orphans, and chancery court—will designate a personal representative for you. The court may select a member of your family, a close friend or associate, a complete stranger, or a public official. This depends on state law, the practice and attitude of the court, and the family situation.

The person selected as personal representative will become responsible for your property and for getting it transferred to

those who are entitled to it. First, he will have to pay your
debts and funeral expenses. Then he will have to pay taxes
and the cost of probate itself. Finally, he will distribute your
remaining property to the persons named in your will or if
you have failed to leave a will, to relatives specified by state
law. If you don't write a will, the state has written one for
you. If you die with no will and no family members surviving,
the state declares itself the sole beneficiary of your estate.

DO YOU WANT YOUR PROPERTY PROBATED?

There is one big advantage. You keep unfettered dominion
over your property while you are alive. The alternative
methods of transferring your property require at least temporary surrender over your property, and that surrender must
still be in effect at the moment of death. Most people don't
like to give up their property, and that is why most people
don't avoid probate.

Still, the probate process entails these disadvantages:

1. The disposition of your property becomes a matter of
public record and anyone can find out what you owned,
whom you owed, and how your property was distributed.

2. Your property is tied up for all or part of the probate
period. This may cut off funds needed by your family, although this hardship can be avoided by will provisions.

3. Your personal representative, who won't know as much
about your property as you do, will have to collect it. An
arrangement made before death offers the advantage of your
knowledge of the things you own. Still, proper instructions in
a letter to your family can largely, if not completely offset
this disadvantage.

4. Making details about your property a public record may
encourage claims against your estate.

5. Your estate will have to pay fees to your personal representative and his legal advisor. True, even when you transfer your property away during your life, there will be some of the same costs, notably the services of your trustee and his legal advisor in settling tax and other claims. But these are likely to be somewhat less than probate costs.

6. The probate court may be required by state law to designate appraisers and guardians to protect the interests of minor beneficiaries of your estate. Naturally, the appointees' fees will be paid out of your estate.

7. Taxes can only be avoided or reduced by the complete surrender of your property during your life, unless your estate isn't big enough to use up its exemptions.

SIX ALTERNATIVES TO PROBATE

This book will examine these alternative methods of transferring property at death:

1. Create a revocable trust to hold or distribute your property at death or specified times after death.

2. Give your property outright to your family or others during life.

3. Transfer your property to an irrevocable trust during your life.

4. Transfer property to members of your family or others in return for their promise to make annual payments to you for life. This is known as the private annuity method of property transfer.

5. Put your real estate, securities, or bank account in joint ownership so that on death the property is owned by the surviving owner or owners.

6. Use some of your property to buy life insurance policies payable on your death to persons named in the policies.

TWELVE WAYS TO COMBINE
THE AVAILABLE TRANSFER METHODS

To transfer his property, a man can use these six methods in an almost infinite number of combinations. A will can direct the disposition of insurance proceeds payable to an estate. Insurance proceeds may be payable to a trust. Bequests in trust may be made by will. Gifts may be in trust or they may take the form of insurance contracts. Trusts may fund insurance premiums.

Here are the more commonly used methods and combinations of methods of transfer that you can use:

1. Keep all your property until death, and then give it all outright to your spouse, who in turn transfers the property to your children by will.

2. Give your property to a trust by will, with income to go to your spouse for her life and with property to go to your children automatically on her death.

3. Will one-half of property outright to your spouse and the remainder, after taxes and costs, to your children.

4. Will one-half of your property to a so-called marital deduction trust with the income payable to your wife for life, she being given a so-called appointment over the principal (right to say who is to have it on her death), and the remainder, after taxes and other costs, to a trust with income to wife for life and the principal to your children on her death.

5. Same as method No. 4 except that income of the second trust goes to your children, either being accumulated for them during their minority or used for their support or distributed to them. To compensate your widow for the loss of income from the second trust, you may give your trustee the power to use all or part of principal if she needs it.

6. Set up a revocable trust, which achieves the objectives of any of the five methods listed above while retaining full flexibility for you to change your mind and utilize the property transferred to the trust, for your own purposes during the remainder of your life.

7. Property transferred during your lifetime to an irrevocable trust may be made immune from estate taxes at the cost of some gift taxes.

8. Property may be transferred via a combination of revocable and irrevocable trusts.

9. Gifts made during your life to your children will take the gift property out of your taxable estate. If the gifts exceed the gift tax exemption ($60,000 for a husband and wife) and the annual exclusion ($6,000 a year to each donee for husband and wife), there will be a gift tax, but it will be in the lower portion of the gift tax scale rather than in the higher portion of the estate tax scale.

10. The shifting of your capital into an insurance contract will, depending on your age, increase the size of your estate and, if the insurance contract is properly placed, the capital transferred, and its increase in value may be shifted outside the impact of the estate tax.

11. All or some of your property can be placed in joint ownership. It will pass to the survivor outside the probate process but the entire value of the property will be subject to estate tax unless your legal representative can show that the survior put up all or part of the investment.

12. You can escape both gift and estate taxes on any property you transfer to a member of your family in return for his or her promise to pay you an annual amount if the amount to be paid, taking into account your life expectancy, is substantially the same as the value of the property transferred.

COMPARATIVE COSTS OF
TWELVE ESTATE TRANSFER METHODS

For illustrative purposes, we will consider a man who is worth $300,000 and show how the net value of his property will vary depending on which of ten methods he selects for the distribution and management of his estate. In calculating transfer costs, we include Federal estate and gift taxes, and State death taxes up to the amount necessary to absorb the credit against Federal estate tax. This is the minimum State tax in most jurisdictions having an estate tax. So its use presents an approximate picture of the overall tax costs. Variations in the application of inheritance or estate taxes of the several states will not significantly alter the arithmetic and will not at all alter the relative merits of the various plans shown.

The estate owner is married (in Method A we assume that he dies a widower). Under the other methods we assume that the wife has no separate estate. Transfer costs exclusive of estate and inheritance taxes are taken at 5 per cent of the gross estate subject to administration. (The numbers in parentheses that follow Methods B to J are references to the twelve methods or combinations of methods that we outlined preceding this discussion of comparative costs.

*% of estate lost in taxes
and administration costs*

METHOD A

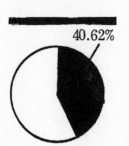

40.62%

Entire estate of an unmarried person passes to a sister or a parent (like surviving spouse, assumed to have no separate estate), then property passes to nieces, nephews, or grandchildren without benefit of marital deductions. Here we have maximum shrinkage. This can happen where a man is unmarried or his wife predeceases him.

24.4%

METHOD B (2)

A man's estate is bequeathed to a trust, with income to his wife for life and property to his children upon her death. Before the 1948 Revenue Act, this was the most economical way to pass an estate. Wills still running this way are apt to be obsolete.

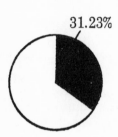

31.23%

METHOD C (1)

All property is willed to a man's wife outright. The wife's will then sends all the property to children. This method qualifies for the marital deduction so that only half the estate is taxed at the husband's death. But upon the wife's subsequent death there's no marital deduction.

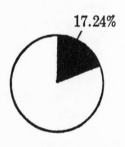

17.24%

METHOD D (3)

A man wills half his property to his wife outright, the other half in trust for his children, possibly with income to his wife for life. Upon his death, half his estate falls subject to tax and all of it to administration costs. Upon his wife's death, the other half is subject to tax and administration costs.

15.53%

METHOD E (4, 5)

A man wills his property to two trusts, one trust qualifying for the marital deduction, the other not. This method has the same tax-saving value as Method D, but saves administration expense upon the second death and provides the wife with professional management of her property.

11.93%

METHOD F (4, 5, 6)

Lifetime transfer of all property to a revocable trust with directions to dispose of property as in Method E, upon deaths of husband and wife. The husband can watch his plan in operation and change the arrangement during his life as circumstances may change or he may decide his original was deficient.

4.13%

METHOD G (7, 8, 9)

Transfer of one-third of property to irrevocable trusts for wife and children. Remaining two-thirds of property is transferred to a revocable trust as in Method F. The transfer to an irrevocable trust may entail gift tax but will take property out of the higher estate tax brackets. Administration costs are saved at the deaths of both husband and wife.

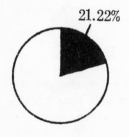

21.22%

METHOD H (10)

A man, age 50, transfers $65,000 of his holdings into a single premium life insurance policy with a face value of $100,000. This increases the estate to $335,000. This transfer method is not strictly comparable with the others because it captures elements of future income and fixes them in the estate. The insurance is owned by the estate owner and made payable to his estate, which is distributed one-half to his wife and one-half to his children; the balance of his property is distributed as in Method E.

21.19%

METHOD I (10)
$65,000 is transferred to an insurance contract as in Method H. But here the insurance is owned by the wife and is included in her estate to be distributed to children. Balance of property distributed as in Method E.

9.87%

METHOD J (4, 5, 7, 10)
$65,000 is transferred to an insurance contract as in Method H. This insurance is assigned by the husband to an irrevocable unfunded insurance trust, the beneficiaries of which are the children. The balance of his property is distributed as in Method E.

28.53%

METHOD K
All property is held in joint ownership and passes to a surviving spouse by operation of law. This produces the same tax effect as Method C but administration costs will be nominal.

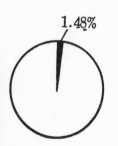

1.48%

METHOD L
All property is transferred to children in exchange for an annuity for joint lives of father and mother. Father, age 65, owns the $300,000 of property and his annuity arrangement constitutes a gift to mother. Mother is also 65. Otherwise, there are no transfer costs.

The following table gives you a breakdown of costs and shows you how we arrived at the percentages of the estate lost in taxes and administration costs.

COST OF 12 METHODS OF TRANSFERRING A $300,000 ESTATE

| | First Death | | Second Death | | After Two Deaths | |
	Expenses of Administration	Estate Tax	Expenses of Administration	Estate Tax	Net Estate Left	Transfer Cost as % of First Estate
Method A	$15,000	$58,200	$11,340	$37,338	$178,122	40.62%
Method B	15,000	58,200	None	None	226,800	24.40%
Method C	15,000	15,800	13,460	49,422	206,318	31.23%
Method D	15,000	15,800	7,125	13,805	248,270	17.24%
Method E	15,000	15,800	None	15,800	253,400	15.53%
Method F	None	17,900	None	17,900	264,200	11.93%
Method G	2,700*	4,800	None	4,800	287,610	4.13%
Method H**	16,750	21,450	2,500	22,950	236,350	21.22%
Method I**	11,750	8,875	5,000	37,950	236,425	21.19%
Method J**	11,862†	8,875	None	8,875	270,388	9.87%
Method K	None	17,900	14,105	53,085	21,491	28.53%
Method L	None	None	None	None	295,575	1.48%

* Gift Tax.
** $65,000 of estate shifted to $100,000 single premium life insurance policy, which increases gross estate to $335,000.
† Includes gift tax of $112.

CHAPTER V

HOW TO SIMPLIFY AND MINIMIZE PROBATE FOR THE SMALL ESTATE

Avoiding probate is an impractical objective. It is awkward, if not silly, to have the title to your automobile held by someone else as a trustee from whom you can snatch back the auto by exercising a power to revoke. But simplifying and minimizing probate is a practical and valuable objective. It is especially desirable for the smaller estate, where probate costs run to a larger percentage of the total property than in larger estates and where probate costs tend to exceed tax costs. For the small estate, the most practical steps to minimize the assets that go through probate are these:

1. Put property in joint ownership.
2. Put title in another party as trustee of a revocable trust.
3. Name individuals or a trustee, *not* your estate, as beneficiary of your life insurance and the death benefits under your pension, profit sharing, or other employee benefit plans.

You have to weigh the cost savings from minimizing probate against any inflexibility or awkwardness in these alternative arrangements.

If the estate is under $120,000, a home, U. S. savings bonds, and other securities can be placed in joint ownership without impairing flexibility, in planning for overall estate tax reduction. If the value of property placed in joint ownership between husband and wife is not much in excess of $60,000, there should be no serious gift tax complications. A good rule of thumb is that any family with prospects of accumulating more than $100,000 will be well advised to put nothing in joint names except the checking account and possibly the home. However, there is a loss of flexibility in disposing of the property to meet family needs. The surviving spouse becomes the sole owner of the property. If the surviving spouse remarries, the new spouse acquires statutory rights. Thus there is a loss of ability to assure that the children will acquire an interest in the property.

Life insurance proceeds and death benefits under employee benefit plans can be kept out of one probate by naming the widow as beneficiary. But these funds are then likely to fall subject to probate when the widow dies. Benefits payable under insurance policies and employee benefit plans can be kept out of probate, and even out of estate tax returns, during the lives of the father, mother, and children by making them payable to a family trust. This trust must be carefully drawn to make the funds available to meet family needs as they develop in the future.

Other property—a family business, securities, income-producing real estate—can be best kept out of probate by transferring title to a trustee under a revocable trust. This preserves adequate control over the property during life and assures that on death the property will become immediately available for family use, as provided in the trust agreement, without going through the probate procedure. However, taxes and the cost of tax proceedings will dip into the trust property if there is enough of it.

ESTATES UNDER $50,000

Where a man has only $50,000 or less in his own name, the chances are he can use a truly simple will leaving everything to his wife. He would want to have a survivorship clause, providing that his wife collects only if she survives him for a fixed period, usually sixty days. If she doesn't survive for that time, then everything is left to their children or to the children of any child who dies before his parents. The survivorship clause means that only the man's estate will have to be probated if both he and his wife die in a common accident (unless, of course, the wife has an estate of her own).

If the unexpected happens and both the man and his wife die at about the same time, in most states the children's share will have to be administered by a court-appointed guardian. Although the court won't be bound by the parents' choice of a guardian, most courts will be strongly influenced by their choice. For this reason, even a simple will should name a guardian for the children. Bear in mind that there are two types of guardians: (1) of the person; and (2) of the property. One person can combine both functions, but it is usually best to name a young, warm, and loving relative as guardian of the person and an older person of financial experience as guardian of the property.

The simple will must, of course, name an executor. Normally, the wife will be named executrix, or co-executrix with a bank, if she survives. Usually, if the wife fails to survive, it will be best to name a bank or local trust company as the executor. One or more family members might also be considered as successor executors. One possible complication in this course is that most states require that executors be residents, and the increasing mobility of our population involves a risk of predicting whether the person named will be a resident when the will takes effect.

ESTATES BETWEEN $50,000 AND $120,000

Where a man has property in his own name worth between $50,000 and $120,000, the chances are he will need something more than the simple will just outlined. If the wife survives for the period named (usually 60 days), the wife will normally be given the entire estate outright. But if she doesn't survive, with this amount of money involved, a trust for the children is feasible and has these advantages over a guardianship:

1. A trustee generally has more flexibility in the investments he can make. Since the fund available will last for a longer period than with a smaller estate, it will be desirable to follow a more diversified investment policy than would be the case for a more limited payout. Probably, common stocks as a hedge against inflation should be bought.

2. In states where trusts are not under court supervision, an out-of-state trustee or co-trustee may be named. This creates added flexibility and may permit the designation of a relative who couldn't act as a guardian even though a court might otherwise be disposed to appoint him.

3. Money not needed for the support of the children during their minority need not be paid over to them when they come of age.

4. A trust permits the property to be distributed to each child according to his need during his minority, depending on the circumstances. This permits the estate to be used more as the parents would have used it if they had lived.

When a trust is used, the trustees should have power to distribute so much of the income and principal as, in their discretion, is necessary for the health, education, and support of the children. This discretion can be limited. One way is to provide that each child receive a proportionate share of the estate at the time the parents die and is limited to the income and principal of his share. Another possibility is a "spray trust," so that the entire principal is available to support all the children until the youngest reaches a suitable age, with the trustees determining how much each. needs. This type of trust has a great appeal.

A spray trust can terminate when the youngest child reaches majority. It may also last longer—for example, until the youngest child reaches 25 years of age or gets a Bachelor's Degree, whichever is earlier. The latter formula cuts off support about the time the parents would stop rather than at an arbitrary age.

Any principal not used for the support of the children, whether each child draws against his own fund or against a common fund, should be distributed to the children when they reach specified ages—21, 25, 30, or older. For estates of the size under consideration, it is doubtful that the trust should continue past 30. The trust should, of course, contain a gift over to the children of any child who dies before distribution is made, or if there are no such children, a gift over to his brothers or sisters. A spendthrift clause may also be included if valid in the state.

The selection of the trustees depends on the family members or friends available. Unless there is a family member or an extremely close friend, it is unwise to have individuals act as the only trustees. Generally the amounts paid to a corporate trustee for acting as co-trustee can be considered money well spent.

When the only beneficiaries are small children, it is usually desirable to have an individual acting as co-trustee. He will have a more personal knowledge of the needs of the children and can help in exercising the discretion entrusted to the trustees over the amount of income and principal to be used each year for the children's health, education, support and maintenance.

The contingent-trust will should also specify an executor and a guardian of the person of the minor children, but the considerations discussed above in connection with the simple will also apply to the selection of these fiduciaries in a contingent-trust will.

ESTATES IN EXCESS OF $120,000

When a man has property in his own name in excess of $120,000, the Federal estate tax considerations become very important. The estate tax is graduated, and the tax on two separate estates is less than the tax on one estate equal in size to the sum of the two smaller estates. A man's estate can be divided into two smaller estates, each the size of half his estate, by the use of the so-called marital deduction. The marital deduction achieves the maximum estate tax saving (assuming the wife has no separate estate of her own) by permitting half the property to be given to the wife in her own name tax-free while the other half is held in a taxable trust for the benefit of the man's family. This plan can be modified by placing the wife's half in a so-called marital trust, but this is desirable in young families only if the wife must be forced to look to someone besides herself for financial guidance.

In a marital deduction will, the trust that does not qualify for the marital deduction—the family trust—usually contains provisions very similar to those suggested above, with two exceptions:

1. The family trust should provide that all the income is to be paid to the wife during her lifetime, together with as much principal as the trustees (other than herself) consider necessary for her health and support, taking into consideration her standard of living and her other resources.

2. She should be given the maximum possible control permitted by the Internal Revenue Code over the principal of the family trust without causing it to be included in her estate. The Code permits her to have two important powers without impairing the tax saving. First, she can be given the right to demand and receive up to 5 per cent of the prin-

cipal of the family trust or $5,000, whichever is greater, in any one calendar year. Second, she may be given a so-called special power of appointment by will over the principal of the family trust. This gives her the power to transfer the principal to individuals within certain special classes defined in the will. Generally this power is limited to the husband's descendants and their spouses.

Giving the wife a large degree of control over the principal without causing the entire principal of the family trust to be included in her estate for Federal estate tax purposes makes her feel that her husband's entire estate is really being used for her benefit. More importantly, it gives her a chance to take a look at the family situation at some time after her husband's death. Perhaps one child has a greater need than another and should have more of the principal than another, or a child may have demonstrated lack of ability to handle money and his trust should last longer than provided for in the husband's will. In any event, it is desirable for the wife to have sufficient control over the family trust to make the necessary adjustments in its provisions as long as this control does not cause the family trust to be included in her estate.

The marital deduction will should include the appointment of executors, guardians of the person of the minor children, and trustees, but the considerations involved in their appointment are similar to those discussed above.

CHAPTER VI

WHAT YOUR ESTATE WILL DO

When you die, here is what will happen to your estate.

1. Your assets have to be collected by your executor.

2. A value must be placed on each asset including any assets you may have placed in the hands of a trustee before your death if you reserved any significant control over or interest in the trust assets. Thus, if you received income from a trust or retained the power to revoke a trust you set up, the assets of the trust must be included in the estate tax return your executor must file.

3. Enough of your assets have to be converted to cash to pay your debts, cash bequests, Federal and State taxes on your estate, attorney's fees, executor's commissions, and other expenses.

Tax returns must be filed and taxes and expenses paid. If your estate is large, taxes will be the big cost. If it is small, expenses will be the big cost. Thus, if you have a million dollar taxable estate, the tax bill will be some $300,000 and expenses some $40,000. If your taxable estate is $80,000, expenses will be in the area of $4,000 and taxes only $1.600.

4. Then the remaining property will be distributed to your beneficiaries. The property available for distribution will not include property held in joint ownership, property held in trust, life insurance proceeds, and employee benefits payable to a beneficiary other than the estate, and any other asset passing outside the will. Nor will this property always be available to pay taxes and expenses, although your executor will usually have to pay taxes on (and incur expenses in connection with) the values they represent.

PROPERTY PASSING OUTSIDE YOUR ESTATE

A large slice of your wealth may very well pass outside your estate. Even though it is taxed as part of your estate, it may not be available to pay cash legacies, debts, expenses, and estate taxes. Property falling into this category will include:

   —real estate, bank accounts, and securities in joint names,
   —insurance you own on your life that is payable to a named beneficiary,
   —death benefits in a pension or profit-sharing plan payable to a named beneficiary,
   —deferred compensation to be continued by your employer to your wife, and
   —life insurance payable under optional modes of settlement, i.e., life-term payments to your wife.

HOW A $500,000 ESTATE CAN GO BANKRUPT

John Jones had $100,000 in securities and a $60,000 home in joint ownership with his wife. He owned $100,000 of life insurance and his company carried $50,000 of group insurance, all payable to his wife. His interest in the company's profit-sharing plan amounted to $90,000. His employment contract required his company to pay his wife $20,000 a year for 10 years. All these interests passed outside his estate. The only assets in his estate were autos and other property worth $10,000 and lands worth $20,000. Yet his estate tax liability was $50,000, and so his estate was bankrupt.

CASH REQUIREMENTS

Cash will be required to pay any legacies specified in your will, as well as estate taxes, debts, doctor and hospital bills, and funeral and administration expenses. We have just seen that the cash for these purposes will not be available from jointly owned property of any kind, life insurance payable to a beneficiary other than the estate, property previously transferred to an irrevocable trust, employee benefits payable to a beneficiary other than the estate—unless arrangements have been made for the recipient of this kind of property to either lend to or to buy assets from the estate.

It is then necessary for you to determine which assets can be converted into the required cash. Each asset must be looked at in terms of its liquidity—the ease with which it can be converted into cash. The values necessary to meet the cash requirements of the estate must be checked off, and only the property remaining after satisfying cash demands will be available to meet family needs.

Here is a schedule you can use to determine cash requirements:

Total Gross Testamentary Assets .... $_____

Non-Testamentary Assets—Subject to Federal
    Estate Tax .... $_____

Executor's Commissions .... $_____

Attorney's Fees .... $_____

Administration Expenses .... $_____

Expenses of Last Illness .... $_____

Funeral .... $_____

Trade Debts .... $_____

    Total Deductions .... $_____

CASH REQUIREMENTS

Debts .... $_____

Federal Estate Tax .... $_____

State Death Tax .... $_____

Cash Legacies .... $_____

Interim Family Requirements .... $_____

TOTAL CASH REQUIREMENTS .... $_____

WHAT WILL BE LEFT FOR FAMILY USE?

After determining the cash requirements, list the assets of your estate and estimate the taxable value and liquid value. They won't be the same; the family business may have high taxable value and very little liquid value. Then mark off enough liquid value to meet the cash requirements and see what is left for family use. Do it this way:

Assets	Taxable Value	Liquid Value	Used to Meet Cash Needs	Remaining for Family Use
Personal Effects	—	—	—	—
Residence	—	—	—	—
Bank Accounts	—	—	—	—
Family Business	—	—	—	—
Bonds	—	—	—	—
Listed Securities	—	—	—	—
Unlisted Securities	—	—	—	—

WHO WILL PAY THE TAXES?

Unless you specify in your will, state law will determine who is responsible for meeting tax obligations. This may mean, for example, that those who receive nothing more substantial than personal effects will be charged with a portion of the tax bill.

The impact of estate and inheritance taxes may be charged against the residuary estate, apportioned, or treated differently as to varying interests. Does the tax fall where you want it and where it will be least felt?

A beneficiary of a gift of real or tangible personal property may have difficulty in paying a proportionate share of the tax without liquidating the gift.

Cash legacies when reduced by a pro rata share of the tax may not be what you intended.

Where there is substantial taxable property passing on

death otherwise than under your will, such as insurance or trusts created during your lifetime, charging all taxes to the residuary estate (what is left after payment of debts, taxes, cash legacies, etc.) under the will, unless contemplated in your testamentary plan, could create difficulties in carrying out that plan.

Here are some questions you and your professional advisers must consider: Where the residuary estate is divided up, is it more advantageous to have one portion bear all the taxes? Where marital deduction is utilized, should taxes be charged to the nonmarital portion? Where there is a percentage gift, is it clear whether it is to be computed before or after taxes?

WHAT WILL YOUR ESTATE DO FOR YOUR FAMILY?

The end purpose of your estate planning is to provide the maximum security, capital, and income for your family. To see what estate tax and other transfer costs will do to your estate, what will be left after these obligations have been paid, what we can do to reduce the obligations, and what we can do to increase the liquid assets available to meet them, take these steps:

(1) Make up a list of assets, this way:

Asset	Market Value	Cost	Taxable Value	Liquidity Value
House	—	—	—	—
—100 shs. XYZ Corp.	—	—	—	—

(2) Estimate total liabilities, this way—

Notes and other debts	—
Estimate of current bills	—
Estimate of income tax liability	—
Medical expenses	—
Funeral expenses	—

(3) Analyze cash needed this way—

	Full Marital* Deduction	No Marital Deduction
Debts	—	—
Funeral and administration expense	—	—
Death taxes, state	—	—
Death taxes, federal	—	—
Cash bequests	——	——
TOTAL CASH NEEDED		

(4) Determine liquidity this way—

Cash needed	—
Liquid assets	——

(5) Project a tentative plan for meeting any liquidity deficit this way—
Amount of deficit overcome by—
Reducing liabilities:
    Lifetime family gifts   —
    Charitable gifts, etc.   —
Increasing cash:
    Additional life insurance   —
    Lifetime sales, etc.   —

(6) Project the estate left for the family, this way—
    Total estate   —
    Total cash obligations   —
        NET FOR FAMILY   —

(7) Project income available for family, this way—
    NET ASSETS available for family   —
        Deduct value of assets that do not produce income and will not be sold and converted into income-producing assets   —
        Deduct lump sum obligations, i.e., college costs   —
        Deduct total amount of any invasions of capital estimated during first . . .** years—

(8) TOTAL INCOME-PRODUCING CAPITAL   —
    Annual income produced by family capital
        At . . . . . .%   —
        At . . . . . .%   —
        On annuity basis   —

---

* The marital deduction is explained in Chapter VIII.
** Whatever period is meaningful in the circumstances.

CHAPTER VII

HOW TO INCREASE YOUR ESTATE

Here we are dealing with ways to create new assets. In the next chapter, we show you ways to reduce liabilities. These are the two roads toward improving your family's position. We will deal only with ways to rearrange your existing assets and income to create larger value at death. You will have to figure out for yourself how to improve your income and sky-rocket the value of your investments.

There are only three ways to increase your estate by re-arranging what you now have:

1. Get your employer to make available to you compensation methods that will generate capital—or get a new job where such opportunities are available, or if you're self employed, set up a self-employed retirement plan—a Keogh plan.

2. Use some of your income or capital to buy life insurance.

3. Shield your investment income from annual tax to accelerate its accumulation into additional capital.

THE PAYROLL ESTATE

Most American corporations have installed capital-generating compensation plans to hold their key employees. Head-hunters roam the land to lure talented executives from companies that do not have such plans to those that have.

What types of plans are available? What kind of capital-generating compensation plans can be created? Remember, we are looking for future capital to provide retirement security and family security at death. It is difficult to create the necessary capital because it can't be shifted or tax-sheltered as investment income can and because that portion of the annual compensation that exceeds annual living expenses gets taxed at the highest rates. So, there are these broad approaches:

1. Have some of the compensation for the job put into a pension or profit-sharing plan where 100 per cent of the dollars put to your credit can be invested to accumulate future capital.

2. Defer some of your compensation in the hope that you and your family will be able to take it down at lower tax rates in future years.

3. Have the deferred compensation invested in company stock in the hopes that ou will enjoy appreciation not only on what would otherwis ᵉ be your savings but also on what would otherwise be the ʟax on the amount of compensation deferred.

4. Get some of your compensation in the form of options on your employer's stock. This will give you a chance to add to your estate at capital gains' rates.

5. Get your employer to carry insurance on your life. This will not only save you the premium money but also the tax on the additional compensation you would need to get the premium money.

The possibilities for adding to your estate via the payroll route break down into: (1) those methods that can be made available to you or any other employee alone; and (2) those methods that only work if they are made available to a broad group of employees.

The following methods are available only to a broad cross section of employees:

1. Pension plan—works best for those with long service and advanced age.

2. Profit-sharing plan—works best for younger employees who will stay on and benefit additionally as others leave and forfeit moneys accumulated to their account.

3. Stock-purchase and thrift-plan benefits can be concentrated among those able and willing to save from their own income.

4. Group insurance—can be purchased in larger denominations for higher paid executives if in accordance with Treasury regulations.

These methods can be made available to one or a small group of executives:

1. An individual deferred compensation contract, which gives the executive cash payments on retirement.

2. An individual deferred comper sation contract, in which the deferred amount is credited in company stock and paid out with credit for dividends and appreciation on the stock to time of payment.

3. Option to buy company stock at present prices at any time during the next five years.

4. The right to buy company stock and pay for it over a period of years—with or without the assurance that the company will buy it back at death on a basis (the then market or a formula value) that will presumably result in a higher price.

5. Split-dollar insurance carried by the executive on his family but carried primarily with funds advanced by the employer as a loan against cash values.

6. Contractual obligations to make payments to the family for some period of years after the death of an employee. This has the same effect as life insurance and the obligation can be funded by policies carried by the company on the employee's life, or payments may merely be made out of the

employer's till as the obligations mature monthly. The payments are deductible to the employer, and this arrangement is one of the easiest methods of creating an instant estate.

SELF-EMPLOYED RETIREMENT PLANS

The Keogh law is a great boon to the self-employed—doctors, lawyers, accountants, contractors, merchants, businessmen, commission salesmen, and all others in business for themselves as individuals. All self-employed individuals can set up their own retirement plans which may enable them to get as much in the way of tax shelter and capital build-up as corporate executives and employees covered under corporate pension or profit-sharing plans.

A Keogh plan gives the self-employed a chance to boost retirement income without cost and, in some cases, the chance to buy retirement income for his wife and other close relatives with 100% deductible tax dollars. It can also bring him greater earnings through the greater incentive and improved performance of covered employees.

Advantages—Here is a checklist of some of the basic advantages which a Keogh plan provides:

(1) The self-employed can contribute up to $2,500 each year on his own behalf.

(2) The self-employed receives an income tax deduction for the full amount he contributes on his own behalf *(for taxable years beginning after December 31, 1967)* and for the full sum he contributes on behalf of his employees. Thus, for example, if an individual contributes the maximum of $2,500 on his own behalf, he will be allowed the full $2,500 as a deduction and, assuming he is in the 50% tax bracket, he would cut his tax bill by $1,250 each time he contributes that sum. Contributions for employees work the same way.

(3) If he has any full-time employees, he may include them in the plan and provide retirement benefits for them also. (Where the employees have worked for the self-employed for three years or more, he must include them.) And he must pay on behalf of his employees the same percentage of their earnings as he does for himself.

(4) A wife who works for her husband may be considered an employee provided she is controlled and directed by the self-employed in the work which she performs and provided that she puts in the required time to be covered by the husband's Keogh plan—i.e., 20 hours a week.

(5) All realized earnings within the plan are permitted to accumulate tax free. This tax protection permits a tax-free compounding of income increments during the period of their accumulation.

(6) A self-employed individual may also contribute on a voluntary basis an additional 10% of his earned income up to $2,500 maximum where he has one or more employees and he extends this same benefit of contributing 10% of salary to the fund on the same voluntary basis as his own contributions. Although neither the self-employed nor the employee is entitled to deductions for these contributions, they still stand to get an important tax benefit by contributing. These funds can be invested and reinvested tax free by the fund, and the accumulation of these tax-free earnings plus the contributions themselves helps build a substantial retirement fund.

(7) The money put into the Keogh plan can be put into all kinds of investments such as stocks, bonds (including special United States bonds), mutual fund shares, real estate, mortgage, etc. The money in the plan can also go to purchase annuities, endowments, and other retirement income-type contracts. See Financing the Plan p. 67.

(8) Although retirement distributions for the self-employed are taxed as ordinary income, he has the benefit of using an averaging formula. Here the tax is five times the increase in tax resulting from adding 20% of the taxable portion of the self-employed's distribution to his other income. But no tax has to be paid on the amounts contributed for which no tax deduction was taken.

Disadvantages—If there is an owner-employee in the plan, then all full-time employees with at least three years' service *must* be covered by the plan too. The employees' rights to contributions made on their behalf must be vested immediately as soon as the contribution is made. Furthermore, there must be no discrimination in the contribution formulas used to determine how much will be contributed for owner-employees and regular employees. The added cost may in a particular case make the plan an added expense, rather than a tax-sheltered vehicle for retirement investment.

In the case of partnerships, only the firm can set up a Keogh Plan, the individual partners cannot set up plans for themselves alone.

Probably the biggest disadvantage of Keogh retirement plans is that once money is committed to the plan it may not be withdrawn prior to age 59½ without severe penalties. So, in effect, the funds are irrevocably committed to the plan once a contribution is made.

How Benefits Can Pyramid—Let's assume you're in a 50% tax bracket and you put $2,500 per year into your Keogh plan. This gives you an annual tax savings of $1,250. You have that much more cash to save. If you invested those savings outside the Keogh plan and got a 4% yield, you'd have accumulated $40,800 after taxes in 25 years. But if you contributed the $1,250 of annual tax savings to your Keogh plan and kept that money invested at 4%, you'd accumulate $54,000 or an additional $13,200.

The basic $2,500 a year, the maximum for which you get a tax deduction, will, at 4%, accumulate to $108,000 in 25 years. Thus, a $2,500-a-year savings plan which, at 4% without Keogh, would accumulate to about $80,000 adds up to $162,000 in a Keogh plan.

In addition, you can tax shelter another $1,250 of voluntary contributions (the maximum voluntary contribution for you is $2,500) which would build up to another $54,000, or an additional $13,200 over what you'd accumulated on a similar investment outside your Keogh plan.

We haven't considered capital appreciation in our investments for the reasons, among others, that a meaningful appraisal would have to take into account the particular investment selected, the price at the time of purchase and the price at the time of sale. A Keogh program geared to investments in securities, common stocks or mutual funds, would necessarily involve periodic investments at different times, and this pattern of investment would give you the effect and the advantage of dollar averaging. Nevertheless, in working out your own program, you will have to take into account the prospect of capital appreciation in the light of your own investment objectives. If, for example, you want to shoot for capital growth and accept the risks that this course entails, the build-up can be very great.

But let's get back to our conservative example. To round out the picture you have to know what happens on the payout end. Of the $216,000 in the kitty, how much will you have after taxes once you start drawing down the benefits? To begin with the $62,500 which you put into the plan by way of voluntary contributions was already taxed and will not be taxed again on withdrawal. That leaves $153,500 which hasn't been taxed. Assuming that this amount comes out an average tax rate of 32% (the $16,000 to $20,000 taxable income tax bracket in 1966), there would be a tax of $49,120, leaving you $166,880.

If you put aside $2,500 per year without a Keogh plan an accumulation of 4% would come out to 2% after taxes. In 25 years you'd have about $80,000. So, via a Keogh plan, the total extra after-tax build up in 25 years would come to about $87,000!

Financing the Plan: You have a choice in setting up your retirement fund—a trust, custodial account, insurance or annuities, or Government retirement bonds.

Trusteed Arrangement: Contributions can be turned over to a bank as trustee. The trustee can then invest the deposits in stocks, bonds, mutual funds, annuities, life insurance contracts, or other investments.

Custodial Arrangement: You can use a bank custodial account instead of setting up a trust. Here, your investments are limited to either (a) mutual funds only, or (b) to annuity, endowment or life insurance contracts only. One custodial account can not invest both in mutual funds and insurance or annuity contracts. But one plan can contain two custodial accounts, one for mutual funds and one for annuities.

Direct Purchase of Annuities: Without interposing either a trustee or a custodian, contributions can be used to purchase annuities (including variable annuities) or face amount certificates. The annuity plan could include either individual contracts or group annuities or both. Either may provide incidental life insurance protection. But the insurance protection must not exceed 100 times the monthly retirement benefit. A typical retirement income policy would satisfy the rule.

Retirement Bonds: Another possibility for setting up a retirement fund is that of using a special retirement bond which the United States Treasury offers. You have to buy the bonds in the name of the individual employee who is covered in your retirement plan. They are not transferable, and may not be sold, discounted or pledged as collateral for a loan. The bonds pay interest at the rate of 3¾% compounded semi-annually but only upon redemption. They can not be cashed until the owner is 59½ years old. The only exceptions are for death or disability.

THE FAMILY INSURANCE INVESTMENT.

There are some fairly decisive priorities that tend to freeze an individual's investment pattern. His first job is to set up capital that would, to some degree, give his family a substitute for his earned income in the event of his death. At the reduced investment yields prevailing today, it takes a lot of capital to even partially replace earning power. Take a $10,000-a-year man who is willing to see his family manage without him on $5,000 a year and to assume a 4 per cent return on money. He has to offset his earning power with $125,000 of capital. The most effective way to do this will be with insurance, and at any age, this will force a great deal of his savings into a dollar investment since no equity forms of insurance are available at this point.

But there are important areas of choice in the form of insurance contracts to be purchased. Do we want pure insurance or do we want an investment combined with insurance? Briefly, term insurance will get in the maximum current protection for the premium dollar. It will release dollars for equity investment. Against this, term insurance inflicts certain risks—a rising insurance cost as we get older, possible uninsurability in later years, and a higher true cost of insurance than in investment type contracts. These are risks and advantages to be pondered very carefully with a qualified life underwriter.

What Can You Do With $100 a Month?

At age 35, for example, $100 a month will buy any of the following:

— $25,000 of 20 year endowment insurance, or

— $25,000 of ordinary life plus $668 a year of equity investment, or

— $55,000 of ordinary life, or

— $55,000 of 20 year term insurance plus $582 a year of investment in investment company shares, or

— $25,000 of ordinary life plus $30,000 of 20 year term plus $330 a year of equity investment.

Various other possibilities are open. In selecting among these alternatives you will have to make many basic decisions such as how much death protection you want, how much you want to save in the insurance contract and how much outside, and how much you want your savings program to depend on automatic and quasi-compulsory requirements and how much on self-discipline.

Now compare these alternatives as to what they can be expected to accomplish in family protection in the event of death, in capital accumulation in 20 years of life, and in continued retirement income.

This comparison is based on actual figures taken from the current rate book of a large, conservative insurance company and from the actual past performance of a large common stock mutual fund. Past performance is, of course, just that, and offers no guarantee of future performance but it can serve as a useful guide in planning your estate.

How Much Death Protection?

The table on the following page will show you how much your family would realize if death occurred during the first 20 years:

VALUE TO FAMILY

Death in	Investment	Endowment Policy	All Ordinary Life	$25,000 Ordinary Life Plus Equity	$25,000 Ordinary Life Plus $30,000 Term Plus Equity	Term Insurance Plus Equity
One year	$ 1,200	$25,000	$55,000	$25,801	$55,396	$55,698
Five years	6,000	25,000	55,000	28,507	56,732	58,055
Ten years	12,000	25,000	55,000	32,147	58,531	61,274
Fifteen years	18,000	25,000	55,000	42,702	63,745	70,423
Twenty years	24,000	25,000	55,000	65,347	74,920	90,152

How Much Capital in 20 Years?

Here are the capital values you would have for retirement at the end of 20 years:

— $25,000 Endowment
— $25,000 Ordinary Life plus equity—$48,997 ($8,650 cash value plus $40,347 of equity)
— $55,000 Ordinary Life—$19,030 cash value
— $55,000 term plus equity—$35,192
— $25,000 Ordinary Life plus $30,000 term plus equity—$28,570

How Much Income Will the Capital Produce?

Assume that the insurance capital is converted to annuity at 55 and the equity capital continues to earn dividends at 5 per cent—about the actual rate of return in the 20th year. Here is how the 5 alternatives compare in capacity to produce retirement income:

Endowment—$1,350 a year
Ordinary Life of $55,000—$1,086 a year
Ordinary Life of $25,000 plus equity—$2,484 a year
Ordinary Life of $25,000 plus $30,000 term plus equity—$1,463 a year
Term of $55,000 plus equity—$1,759.50 a year
Remember that the annuity income on insurance values

consumes capital while the 5 per cent investment yield on equity values does not.

The net of this analysis is that some combination of ordinary life plus equity seems to get the best combination of family death security and retirement income. The relative importance you want to give to family protection as against retirement income can be achieved by the way you decide between equity and term insurance after you have covered your need for permanent insurance protection with ordinary life. There are many ways to do this with family maintenance-type policies and other forms of part term, part permanent insurance, which your insurance adviser can show you.

EIGHT WAYS TO USE INCOME TO BUILD YOUR ESTATE

Very often a person will enjoy high income but have little capital. A similar problem is presented when a very wealthy person has big income, a large estate, but inadequate liquidity. In both cases the problem is to convert highly taxed income into additional liquid capital. Here are possible methods that should be canvassed:

(1) *A funded life insurance trust,* in which income is shifted to the lower tax bracket of the trust and used to buy life insurance and guarantee additional liquid capital on the death of somebody other than the person creating the trust.

(2) *An accumulation trust,* in which income-producing assets are transferred to a trust and income shifted to the lower tax bracket of the trust and accumulated for designated family beneficiaries.

(3) *A short-term trust,* to which income-producing capital is transferred for a limited period of time with the income accumulated for the benefit of your wife and some other

member of your family and the income-producing capital reverts to you when the trust ends.

(4) *Give illiquid assets to a family foundation or other charity* to save income-tax cash, which can then be used to carry life insurance or otherwise build liquid assets.

(5) *Transfer dividend-paying stock* (or other income-producing assets) *into a corporation* where income can be accumulated at lower tax rates.

(6) *Instead of increases in compensation,* get your employer to continue salary payments or other *death benefits to your widow.*

(7) *Get your employer* to finance additional life insurance on a split-dollar basis, the employer paying part of the cost.

(8) *Retain earnings in a corporation* (there is no problem on the first $100,000, but after that the money must be earmarked for use in the business) so that accumulated surplus can be taken out in redemption of stock to pay death taxes and other death costs.

HOW TO ACCUMULATE RETIREMENT CAPITAL VIA A SHORT-TERM TRUST FOR YOUR WIFE

Most states now permit accumulation of trust income for an adult. With this in mind, a unique way to build up a retirement fund is for you to transfer income-producing property to a so-called reversionary accumulation trust for your wife.

Take a man in the 50 per cent tax bracket who expects to retire in around 15 years. He has $60,000 worth of securities, which yield 5 per cent or $3,000 a year. He now retains only $1,500 of this income after taxes. Suppose he sets up a 15-year trust for his wife, deposits these securities therein, and empowers the trustee to accumulate the income. When the trust ends, the accumulated income would go to the wife, the trust corpus to the husband.

For the sake of illustration, assume that the income remains stable at $3,000 a year, and that at the end of the 15-year period, the value of the trust property still remains at $60,000. Without the trust, $22,500 ($1,500 a year for 15 years) would have been accumulated, which when added to the $60,000 original capital, would provide a retirement fund of $82,500. With the trust it is possible to accumulate around $2,500 each year, or $37,500 after 15 years. Adding this to the $60,000 original capital would provide a retirement fund of $97,500— some $15,000 more than could have been accumulated without the trust. And this is without taking into account the more rapid build-up of the accumulation because of the trust's lower tax bracket.

Whereas the accumulated income goes to the wife, it is still the family unit getting the benefit of these extra accumulations.

With an arrangement such as this there is the possibility, depending on the size of the gift of income, that there may be a gift tax to pay when the trust is set up. Of course, the estate owner can apply his lifetime exemption and gift tax marital deduction to reduce or even eliminate any tax that might otherwise be payable. In any event, the income tax savings should more than offset any gift tax.

CHAPTER VIII

HOW TO REDUCE ESTATE LIABILITIES

There are really only three ways to substantially reduce estate liabilities. One is to take full advantage of the so-called marital deduction. This will free up to one-half your estate from tax if that portion is bequeathed for the benefit of the surviving spouse in the right way.

The second main method is to suspend ownership and give a prime beneficiary an interest that will not be taxed a second time on his death. You do this when you put your property in trust, give your wife a life interest, and let the property go to your children when your wife dies. This skips the tax on your wife's death.

The third method is to transfer property during life by gift or by some other transaction with a member of the family so that it will not be includable in your estate.

MARITAL DEDUCTION

The marital deduction is by far the most important deduction in the estate tax law and the most important opportunity to reduce the estate bill and the cash requirement at death. The law exempts property going to a surviving spouse provided it is received in such a manner that what is left when the surviving spouse dies will be subject to estate tax. It makes one-half your estate exempt from taxes provided it goes to your surviving spouse, either outright or in a trust that qualifies for the marital deduction. A trust for the benefit of your spouse for her life with the remainder interest going to her estate or being subject to a so-called general power of appointment, giving her the right to say who is to get the remainder, will qualify for the marital deduction. On the other hand, a property interest that is terminable during the surviving spouse's lifetime or where the interest at the death of the spouse passes automatically to children or to other named beneficiaries will not qualify for the marital deduction. Thus, all that you have to do to exempt one-half your estate from taxes is to let your wife determine where it is to go on her death—to children, to grandchildren, to a second husband, or to someone else. You can tie up the property during your wife's life so that she can't squander it, without losing the tax exemption, provided you let her have the annual income and let her determine who is to get the property on her death. You can even require that the income be accumulated during her life so long as you make her estate the beneficiary of the trust. The income of the marital deduction trust will be taxed to such a trust or to your wife, whoever gets the money. Your wife can be authorized to withdraw during her life as much of the principal of the marital deduction trust as your will or trust instrument creating it allows. Property that you own jointly with your wife and insurance passing to her outside the estate will also qualify for the estate tax exemption given by the marital deduction. If you don't want your wife to have the benefits and powers listed above, your executors will have to pay tax on all your property.

The cash savings in qualifying for the marital deduction are substantial. For example:

Size of Estate	Savings
$ 100,000	$ 4,800
200,000	26,700
300,000	41,600
400,000	56,200
500,000	71,200

AVOIDING MULTIPLE ESTATE TAXES

When property is left outright to your children, it will again fall subject to tax when on their death it passes to your grandchildren. When property in excess of the marital deduction (more than one-half your estate) is left to your wife, the excess will be taxed a second time on her death.

This double tax may be mitigated by a credit for property previously taxed as part of your estate. But this credit is reduced by 10 per cent each year after your death and so entirely disappears after ten years. This multiple tax can be avoided by setting up a trust that gives your children (or your wife, for property in excess of the marital deduction) only a life interest with the remainder interest going to the succeeding generation. The security of the life beneficiaries can be further provided for by giving your trustees discretionary power to make distributions out of capital when needed and by giving the life beneficiaries power to make limited withdrawals from the principal. In addition to the annual income, the beneficiaries can withdraw up to 5 per cent of principal or $5,000 each year without losing the tax benefits of this arrangement. The tax savings available in this arrangement must be weighed against the tying up of the property for the life of the beneficiaries. The strings may deprive them of economic opportunity; on the other hand, they may save them from dissipating their capital.

The cash savings from the suggested trust are:

Gross Estate	Cash Savings
$100,000	$ 4,800
200,000	26,460
300,000	39,430
400,000	61,336
500,000	63,536

TRANSFERRING PROPERTY OUT
OF YOUR ESTATE

This is the third method of reducing estate liabilities. There are two ways to do this:

(1) By gift, provided you're in good health so that the gift won't be considered "in contemplation of death." Actually, even if a gift is "in contemplation of death," the property still escapes estate tax if you live for three more years. You and your wife can give $6,000 to *each* child and each grandchild or other person each year free of gift tax. In addition, you and your wife can give another $60,000 tax free during your lifetime.

The gift tax has three other advantages over the estate tax:

(a) The rate runs only three-quarters of estate tax rates.

(b) The estate tax rates apply to the gross estate, including the money needed to pay the estate tax. The gift tax applies only to the net gift and not to the tax cost of the gift.

(c) When property is given, it comes off the top estate tax bracket and goes over to start at the bottom of the graduated gift tax brackets.

(2) By selling property to a member of the family. The price has to be at full value or the difference is a taxable gift. The estate planning advantage of this kind of transaction is that future appreciation in value escapes estate tax, future income may fall into the lower tax brackets, and accumulated income escapes estate tax. Thus, installment sales and sale-leasebacks (you sell business property, for example, but continue in possession under a lease) by a father to a son, the creation of a family partnership or a

family corporation, and the transfer of property for a promise to make annual annuity payments, can be effective estate-planning steps.

ELEVEN WAYS TO MAKE
LIFETIME TRANSFERS OF PROPERTY

(1) Gifts—can be made tax-free up to $3,000 a year to each donee, plus an additional $30,000 (double this if a spouse joins in the gift); beyond that the gift tax rates are only three-quarters of the estate tax rates, gift property is taken from the top estate tax brackets to start at the bottom of the gift tax brackets, and the gift tax is based on the net value of the gift (not including gift tax liability) while estate tax is based on the gross estate including the estate tax liability.

(2) Private Annuities—by which property is tranferred in exchange for the promise of the transferee to make annual payments over the balance of the transferor's life. There is no estate tax on this transfer and no gift tax if the annual payments are in line with the commerical annuity that can be purchased with the value of the property transferred. There is no capital gains' tax until the annual payments received by transferor exceed the cost of the property. The transferee gets no deduction for the annual payments made.

(3) Family Partnership—in which an interest can be acquired by another member of the family either by gift or by purchase so that future income and increments of value will accrue to his benefit.

(4) Family Corporation—in which preferred and common stock can be distributed to family members either by gift or by purchase so that accumulation of income and appreciation in property value will accrue to the common

stockholders. Investment companies will have to avoid personal holding company status.

(5) Life Income Charitable Gift—in which property is transferred to a charity or a trustee for a charity with income reserved for the life of the transferor, specified members of his family, or others, after which the property goes to charity. This is a method of transferring future income to other members of the family at an actuarially reduced gift tax cost, which is offset by the income-tax deduction for the actuarial value of the remainder of the interest. The deduction is not available, however, where the property transferred consists of art objects or other items of tangible personal property. It is freely available for gifts of securities or real estate. It can make it possible to shift investments without capital gains' tax. The life interest passing to the others will be subject to estate tax on the transferor's death, but at actuarially reduced values. This will increase the amount of other property that can go to a spouse tax free under the marital deduction to offset estate tax on the additional life interest.

(6) Deferred Charitable Gift—in which property is transferred to a charity or to a trustee for a charity with income for the benefit of the charity for a specified period of years or for the life of the transferor, with the property then reverting to named members of the transferor's family. This actuarially reduces the size of the taxable gift and gives remainder beneficiaries the property plus any appreciation tax free. It also gives the transferor a current income-tax deduction in the amount of the actuarial value of the income reserved for the charity.

(7) Installment Sale—selling property to members of the family for a small down payment plus installment obligations shifts income and future appreciation to the buyer. Set the terms of the transactions realistically to avoid possible im-

position of gift tax on any bargain elements of the deal. You will need technical advice to make sure you don't run afoul of the imputed interest rules, which can disqualify an installment sale.

(8) Sale-Leaseback—between members of the family can shift rental income and future appreciation. Again set realistic figures for the price and rent to avoid possible gift tax.

(9) Funded Life Insurance Trust—in which you place income-producing property in trust to carry life insurance on somebody other than yourself. This shifts income and assures its future accumulation into capital that will accrue to the beneficiaries named in the trust.

(10) Salary Continuation Agreements—in which your employer is committed to make continued payments to your widow. These payments, if kept in reasonable line with the value of your services during your life, can shift substantial value to your wife or children; these values will be supported by payments that your employer can deduct; and the estate tax, if any, will be based on the actuarially computed value of the future payments at the time of your death.

(11) Split-Dollar Insurance—in which your employer can advance part of the money needed to carry insurance policies for you (at a small tax cost to you) or any member of your family can advance part of the money needed to carry an insurance policy for another member of the family, with the result that the windfall profit of the insurance would accrue to the benefit of the beneficiary named in the policy.

CHAPTER IX

HOW TO SET UP YOUR ESTATE NOW

Your estate can be substantially set up, and you can see it in action by establishing a revocable living trust now. You transfer ownership of some or all of your investment and business-type assets to this trust and supplement it with a simple will that simply "pours over" your remaining assets to that trust. This revocable trust is a substitute for a will or as a professional estate planner would say, an alternative method of testamentary disposition. It is an "inter vivos" (lifetime) transfer, which can be recalled or changed.

During your lifetime, you are able to exert a large measure of control over your property and if you wish, have the beneficial enjoyment of it. The plans you made for its disposition upon your death may be modified from time to time as changing circumstances make such modifications desirable, either by revoking the trust and creating a new one or by exercising retained powers to alter or amend. Thus, you may add, remove, or substitute beneficiaries; change the nature of their interests; change the powers of the trustee; and augment, diminish, or change the trust property. Moreover, during your life you will have the sense of security that your retained power to revoke and have the trust property returned to you inevitably brings. You need never experience the bitter frustration of suddenly needing property you have previously irrevocably conveyed.

Yet, upon your death none of the property in trust will be part of your probate estate. The advantages of avoiding probate are often very real. These advantages, combined with the flexibility that you retain during your lifetime, make the so-called inter vivos revocable trust a workable substitute for a will. Property also may be kept out of your probate estate by an irrevocable transfer made during your lifetime. But once an irrevocable conveyance is made, flexibility is lost. The revocable trust combines some of the advantages of an irrevocable inter vivos conveyance with some of the advantages of retention of property until death.

Reduction of fees and simplification of property transfer are the major advantages of a revocable living trust. Estate and income-tax status remains unchanged, and there is no gift tax. But the assets placed in the revocable trust are not included in the probate estate on which the executor and the lawyer for the estate calculate their fees. This saving is reduced by two factors:

(1) The extra or special fee that will be charged for filing the estate tax return, handling the estate tax audit, and other duties arising from the inclusion of trust assets in the taxable estate.

(2) The cost of establishing and operating the trust for the duration of your life. This charge is deductible. You may obtain valuable custody and investment services from the trustee for these charges; if you don't need them, you may be able to negotiate a lower trustee fee during your life. There may be additional fees for revoking the trust or withdrawing property. These are matters on which you should have a clear and explicit understanding with the trustee.

The major administrative advantages come from bringing the assets together and placing title in the trustee so that you settle the applicable law, avoid ancillary administration (if assets are scattered, you may need administration in two or more places), put the trustee in command as soon as you die, and avoid interruption of income at death or if you should become incompetent.

The advantages of a revocable living trust may be conveniently listed as follows:

(1) Since you have retained the power of revocation, you control the property and can alter the gift to make it conform to changing needs and circumstances.

(2) You can delegate the burdens of management to an expert—the trustee.

(3) The continuance of a going business is guaranteed even though you die or become incapacitated.

(4) Interruption in family support due to your death or incapacity is avoided.

(5) You can observe the trust in operation and can resolve any ambiguities or difficulties that arise.

(6) The expenses and delays of probate are avoided.

(7) Since it is not part of your probate estate, it is not subject to public scrutiny.

(8) If you own realty or tangible personal property located in another state, ancillary administration may be avoided by placing the property in a revocable living trust.

(9) You can select the law governing the trust with greater ease than if it is done by will.

(10) Because of statutory restrictions on gifts to charities by will (which exist in some states), a charity is more certain to receive its gift if a revocable inter vivos trust rather than a will is used, since restrictions are inapplicable to the revocable inter vivos trust.

(11) The trustee of such a trust may be designated as the beneficiary of a life insurance policy or a pension or profit-sharing plan. Many insurance companies are reluctant to make benefits payable to a trustee named in a will.

Remember, if you want to keep pension benefits out of your taxable estate, they must go to a named beneficiary or to a living trust.

(12) The trustee of a revocable inter vivos trust may be authorized to use insurance proceeds to buy assets at a fixed price from your executor so as to obviate the necessity of your executor selling assets at a depressed value to pay debts and taxes.

(13) Since it is a transfer made during your lifetime, it is easier to rebut efforts to set your plans aside on the grounds of incapacity, duress, or fraud.

(14) Since it is a noncourt trust, it has greater freedom (both as to accounting and other administrative problems) than a will-created trust.

(15) Assets may be poured over from a will to the trust and disposed of in accordance with the terms of the revocable inter vivos trust.

(16) In some states, a surviving spouse cannot satisfy her statutory-forced share out of property in a revocable inter vivos trust.

(17) In some states, your creditors (in the absence of a fraudulent conveyance) may not be able to reach property that you have transferred to a revocable inter vivos trust.

CHAPTER X

JOINT OWNERSHIP AND COMMUNITY PROPERTY

There are three ways to hold ownership in common or joint names:

(1) *Tenancy in common*—Each owns undivided interest in the property. Each may sell his own portion. Heirs of each take portion of each. It just means that when A dies, his half interest isn't forfeited to B. It belongs to A's heirs or passes according to his will.

(2) *Joint tenancy*—All of the property passes to the survivor on death of one. While they are both alive, either joint owner can usually break up ownership even against the will of the other joint owner. But if the joint tenancy is not broken up, it is a gamble who will be the survivor and wind up owning the property.

(3) *Tenancy by entirety*—used only by legally married persons. Entire property goes to survivor on death of one. Neither may sell without approval of other. Cannot exist after a divorce—all property previously held this way is assumed to be held as tenants in common—each holds undivided interest. This is in effect a special kind of joint tenancy between husband and wife, recognized only in certain states. Survivor takes all, and unlike the ordinary joint tenancy, neither party can break it up without the consent of the other.

JOINT TENANCY

A joint tenancy is a simple and convenient way to own property. When one joint tenant dies, the property automatically passes to the survivor. When your spouse is the other joint tenant and this happens, the property qualifies for the marital deduction—thus saving estate taxes. In addition, probate and administration expenses as well as red tape are avoided because the property passes directly to the survivor.

Because of this, the temptation to put all your property in joint tenancy instead of making a will is strong indeed—especially where the estate is not a large one. Small wonder, then, that the joint tenancy arrangement has been referred to as the "poor man's will." Still, joint tenancies certainly do not present an unmixed blessing even for the "poor" man. Whereas, as we have seen, they offer some advantages, they suffer from some very definite disadvantages. This is true from the point of view of family protection and the saving of taxes. These considerations should make us take a long hard look at this so-called "poor man's will."

Let us look at both the family protection and tax consequences of joint ownership of property so that we may be better able to evaluate this type of arrangement. First, we'll look at how the inflexibility of joint ownership frequently makes it a poor substitute for a will, then at the gift tax consequences, and the estate tax and other consequences. Then we'll consider the different ways in which joint ownership can be unwound.

WEAKNESSES AS COMPARED T,O WILL

The very fact that jointly owned property automatically passes to the survivor when one joint tenant dies means that the property passes regardless of the will of the joint tenant who is the first to die. Although the survivorship element that attaches to joint ownership performs the same title-passing function as a will, it doesn't have the flexibility of a will.

Through your will you can provide for any number of changes in your family situation that may require different temporary or permanent uses of the property. You cannot do this if you base your estate planning on survivorship. Survivorship also doesn't provide a way of making sure that the property will be available to satisfy the specific needs of minors, invalids, incompetents, and other loved ones who may require unusual treatment. It doesn't provide a method of dealing with a spendthrift, and it offers no general assurance that the property will be managed responsibly.

Joint ownership of property can lead to unexpected results. For example, a man who has children by his first and second wives who places property in joint ownership with his second wife cuts off the children of his first marriage, at least so far as that property is concerned.

Again, suppose you and your wife are in an accident. You are killed immediately, your wife survives you but not long enough to make a will. What happens to the jointly owned property? It would go to your in-laws, if you have no children, to the exclusion of your heirs.

GIFT TAX CONSEQUENCES

Generally, when you put property owned by you into joint ownership you make a gift of half that property to your co-owner. Also, if you later have a change of heart and put it back in one name, there is another gift—even if the recipient is the one who bought and paid for the property in the first place. Although bank accounts, a residence, and U. S. savings bonds are not ordinarily treated as gifts for tax purposes at the time when they are placed in joint ownership, they are dealt with as gifts by IRS when they are cashed in, if the proceeds go to the one who didn't pay for them or if they are put in that person's name.

In any case, not all gifts are taxed. For example, if you make a gift to your wife, half that gift is exempt. Likewise, all household money is also exempt. In addition, you can make tax-free gifts to the tune of $3,000 a year per person to as many persons as you wish, plus another $30,000 during your lifetime (called the "lifetime exemption"). And if you and your wife make the gifts, the amounts are doubled, even though you own the property given.

What this boils down to is that you are most likely to get stuck for gift taxes if you have large amounts of property in joint ownership. Gift taxes can add up to a tidy sum down through the years, especially since gifts are figured cumulatively throughout your lifetime in determining which rates apply.

ESTATE TAX CONSEQUENCES

When you die, jointly owned property is included in your estate, except to the extent that it originally belonged to the survivor and wasn't acquired from you for less than full value. In other words, only the part contributed or paid for by the survivor can be excluded from your estate for estate tax purposes. In figuring your estate tax, IRS presumes that everything you held in joint ownership belonged to you. Your personal representatives can overcome this presumption by showing how much the survivor contributed—but they will have a hard row to hoe when they try to do this, especially if the survivor is your wife. What is even worse is that the property is taxed again when the survivor dies, since the survivor is the sole owner of the property. And if the property remains intact, it will be included in full in the survivor's estate. The marital deduction won't be available unless your widow has taken another husband who survives her.

However, bear in mind that as we have already stated, if the estate is under $120,000, a home, U. S. savings bonds, and other securities can be placed in joint ownership without impairing flexibility, in planning for overall estate tax reduction. If the value of property placed in joint ownership between husband and wife is not much in excess of $60,000, there should be no serious gift tax complications. A good rule of thumb is that any family with prospects of accumulating more than $100,000 will be well advised to put nothing in joint names except the checking account and possibly the home.

INCOME TAX CONSEQUENCES

When you put income-producing property in joint ownership, each joint tenant reports his proportionate share of the income. But because of the income-splitting rules, this rule doesn't apply if you put the property in joint ownership with your wife.

Income after one of the joint tenants dies is taxable entirely to the survivor.

HOW TO UNWIND JOINT OWNERSHIP

If you already have property in joint ownership and you want to regain flexibility in disposing of the property by unwinding the joint ownership, there are five ways of accomplishing this:

(1) Switching full title back to the estate owner alone.

(2) Switching the title so as to eliminate the estate owner altogether.

(3) Switching to a tenancy in common.

(4) Exchange of properties when there are two or more held in joint ownership.

(5) Sale of his interest in the property by estate owner to the other owner.

Each of these methods of untangling joint ownership is fraught with income tax, gift tax, estate tax, and legal snarls. Consideration must be given to the type of asset jointly owned, to the date the joint ownership was created, and above all, to the objectives of the joint owners. Thus, this is an area that requires the application of professional skill and experience to all the facts in order to produce an analysis of all the alternatives and their implications.

Home: It will probably not be a good idea to transfer your residence to the sole ownership of one of the joint tenants. The transfer would cost money in legal fees. Furthermore, if you alone paid for the house and you now put it in your wife's sole name, your estate might be taxed on it anyway because IRS would claim that since you continued to live in the house, you never gave up your interest in it.

Bank Accounts: You may want to keep bank accounts in joint ownership. But keep some money in separate accounts also so that you won't have to get a release from your state tax authorities when the survivor needs funds.

COMMUNITY PROPERTY

While community property concepts are of primary importance to residents of community property states, they might also come to the fore in noncommunity property states. This is especially true today as more and more families move from one state to another.

Example: John and Mary Jones live in New Mexico. John buys XYZ stock in his name with community funds. This stock becomes community property under New Mexico law. Then they move to New Jersey. Do the shares now become John's separate property? No—that which was community property in the state of acquisition does not change in status merely by being carried into another state where it would have been separate property if acquired there. (Reversing the situation, suppose John and Mary move from New Jersey to New Mexico after the shares have been purchased in John's name in New Jersey. Applying the same reasoning as above, John's separate property would not now automatically become transformed into community property.)

Property acquired by husband and wife during marriage while residing in Arizona, California, Idaho, Louisiana, Nevada, New Mexico, Texas, or Washington is generally community property, and the income therefrom is community property also.

Community property laws do not apply to property that belonged to either spouse at the time of the marriage, or to property acquired after marriage by means of gift, devise, or descent. This remains separate property. Also, it is generally possible for spouses to agree that certain of their property is not to be community property. For example, in some, though not all, community property states, it is possible for a husband and wife to have title to property as joint tenants if they so desire.

It is important to realize that the laws of the several community property states differ in many respects. Although all community property states make the earnings of spouses during marriage community property, only some apply the same treatment to damages for personal injuries. While income, profits, and improvements relating to separate property of a spouse are held to be community property in some states, they constitute separate property in others.

In some community property states, upon the death of one spouse, half the community property belongs automatically to the survivor. In at least one, all the community property will vest in the surviving spouse except where there are children, in which case only half of the community property will so vest. In at least one state, although a surviving wife will take automatic title to half the community property, a surviving husband, on the other hand, will take title automatically to all the community property.

Generally speaking, the husband, as manager of the community, usually controls and may even dispose of or exchange community property during the continuance of the marriage.

Here is a brief rundown of some of the more important Federal income, gift, and estate tax treatments of community property:

Income Tax

Community income is taxed one-half to each spouse regardless of whether they file joint or separate returns. At the death of either spouse, the entire community property may get a stepped-up basis, depending on whether at least one-half the property was taxable in the decedent's estate.

Gift Tax

There is no gift made at the time property that is earned or acquired by one spouse automatically takes on the characteristic of community property. There may be a gift where one spouse's separate property is transformed into community property. And note the following:

(1) Where community property is transformed into separate property, there may be a gift (as determined by state law).

(2) Where spouses make an inter vivos gift of community property to a third person, both spouses are subject to the gift tax on the value of their respective half interests.

Estate Tax

Ordinarily, one half the community property is included in the estate of a deceased spouse. For example, if the wife died first, in most community property states one half the community property would be included in her estate despite the fact that her husband alone had earned all the community property. Although the marital deduction specifically does not apply to community property, it is only because community property already has its own marital deduction built into its structure.

CHAPTER XI

HOW TO ARRANGE YOUR LIFE INSURANCE

When you own insurance on your life, the value of the insurance protection to your family is whittled down by the estate tax.

The following table compares the insurance needed to yield a given net estate with and without the policy being owned by the insured and thus includable in the taxable estate:

Net Estate After Any Marital Deduction But Before $60,000 Exemption	Insurance Needed to Pay Federal Estate Taxes If Included in Estate	If Not Included in Estate
$ 100,000	$ 6,154	$ 4,800
200,000	46,714	32,700
300,000	91,912	62,700
400,000	138,971	94,500
500,000	191,846	126,500
750,000	335,737	212,200
1,000,000	505,173	303,500

Even though you pay the premiums, the proceeds of insurance on your life can be protected from the impact of the estate tax. All you have to do is to transfer the policy and all incidents of ownership to your wife or child or to a trust.

To achieve this, you must assign the policy and give up any power over the policy and its benefits. You must give up the right to surrender, pledge, or cancel the policy; to assign the policy or revoke assignment; to borrow on the policy; to change the beneficiary; to select the settlement method. You must be sure that, on an actuarial basis, there is no more than one chance in twenty that the proceeds will revert to your estate because the beneficiaries die before you do.

When you assign a life insurance policy, you make a taxable gift. There will be no gift tax if the value of the policy is less than the unused portion of the $30,000 gift tax exemption ($60,000 for a man and wife) and the $3,000 annual exclusion ($6,000 for man and wife).

The value of the policy for gift tax purposes is the cost of replacing it. This is usually the policy's interpolated terminal reserve, and your insurance man can supply this figure on request.

HOW THE VALUE OF THE INSURANCE IS INCREASED

Here is a table that will give you an idea of how a change in the ownership of an insurance policy can increase every additional net $1,000 of insurance value you can carry for your family:

| | Net Insurance Value | |
Size of Taxable Estate	Before Change	After Change
$ 100,000	$ 1,000	$ 1,300
200,000	1,000	1,400
500,000	1,000	1,500
600,000	1,000	1,550
1,000,000	1,000	1,600
2,000,000	1,000	1,900
5,000,000	1,000	2,700

These calculations have been rounded off with a typical state tax, and you will have to check your own state law to make precise calculations with your own figures.

HOW INSURANCE PAYABLE TO A WIFE
CAN AVOID TAX TO THE
EXTENT OF 50% OF THE ESTATE

The marital deduction is explained in Chapter VIII. To qualify life insurance for the marital deduction, you must insert the following conditions:

(1) The life insurance policies must have been owned by you.

(2) Your wife must be the unconditional beneficiary entitled to the proceeds at the time of your death (this requirement is relaxed in two particulars in the case of common disaster and six-month survivorship clauses).

(3) If the proceeds are not payable outright and a successor beneficiary is required, one of the following two sets of circumstances must be met in order to qualify the proceeds for the marital deduction—

(a) Assurance that no part of any remainder interest goes to anyone other than to your widow or to her estate. This may be done either by eliminating all possibility of a remainder interest or by arranging that the remainder interest passes to your widow or to her estate. Thus, provisions for your widow to receive one lump sum, a straight life annuity, or interest or installments for life all qualify.

(b) The beneficiary provisions meet the following five conditions:

(i) The insurance proceeds shall be held by the insurance company subject to its agreement to pay them in installments or to pay interest thereon and that, as long as your widow lives, all such payments must be unconditionally payable to her and only to her. If all five conditions apply to part of the proceeds of the policy, that amount can qualify for the marital deduction. A spendthrift clause, which shuts off access to the policy proceeds to the claims of creditors and prevents assignment or alienation or pledge, will not result in a failure to meet this condition.

(ii) Interest installment payments must be payable annually or more frequently, beginning not later than thirteen months after your death.

(iii) Your widow must have the power, exercisable in favor of herself or her estate, to appoint all the proceeds held by the insurance company; that is to say, to name the persons who are to get the proceeds. This condition is met if your wife has the right to withdraw the whole or any part of the proceeds held or the right to direct the payment of all the proceeds remaining at her death to her estate. As a practical matter, most insurance companies will allow withdrawal of proceeds held under an interest option; but as to insurance proceeds held under a settlement agreement calling for the payment of installments over a fixed period of time or for life, they will allow only a single withdrawal of the commuted value of all unpaid installments as of the date of withdrawal.

(iv) The power of appointment must be exercisable by your widow and must be exercisable in all events.

(v) *Amounts payable under the policy must not be subject to any power of appointment in part to a person other than the widow.* You can qualify settlement payment plans for the marital deduction either by making the remainder interest absolutely payable to your widow's estate or by giving her a general power of appointment over the remainder interest.

LIFE INSURANCE PROCEEDS PAYABLE TO TRUST

One way to get investment management and control, plus availability of insurance proceeds, to your widow is to have the proceeds made payable to a trust. In this situation, whether or not the insurance proceeds qualify for the marital deduction will depend entirely on the terms of the trust. If it is a trust in which the widow-beneficiary's interest after her death goes to her estate or over which she has a power of appointment *and which in other respects meets the five requirements outlined above,* the proceeds, through the trust, will qualify for the marital deduction.

An important advantage of this method is that it does not require that income be paid at least annually to the wife. Thus, this method may be advantageous in situations where you want to have the payments of the insurance proceeds concentrated in some period beginning more than a year subsequent to the date of death. It permits the accumulation of income from the policy proceeds for payment during some period in the future.

The power of appointment method allows you to name secondary beneficiaries to receive the proceeds left after your wife's death and to determine how they are to get the proceeds, subject to your wife's right to cancel out these arrangements and make other arrangements. Similarly, in most states the power-of-appointment method avoids state inheritance taxes on the remainder interest that would otherwise fall in your wife's estate, assuming that your wife has not exercised her power to bring the remainder proceeds into her estate.

EXERCISE OF SETTLEMENT OPTIONS LEFT TO WIFE

Another way you can qualify the proceeds of insurance on your life for the marital deduction and still get the benefit of settlement options is to refrain from exercising the options yourself, making your beneficiary designation so that your wife is entitled to receive the entire proceeds in a lump sum, leaving it to her to exercise the settlement options. Whether you exercise the optional mode of settlement or leave it for the beneficiary to exercise, the annual payments receive the same income-tax treatment. But the fact that your wife had the right to take down the proceeds in a lump sum would qualify the proceeds for the marital deduction. The fact that she elects an optional mode of settlement is regarded as an investment of the proceeds and won't disqualify the proceeds. The risk is, of course, that your wife may not use the optional mode of settlement. She may take a lump-sum settlement; and if she doesn't know how to handle money, the proceeds may soon be squandered.

WHO SHOULD OWN THE POLICIES

We can avoid estate tax by having someone other than you own the policies insuring your life. You must decide whether this future estate tax saving is worth giving up the cash surrender value of the policy as an asset in your balance sheet. You can, to a degree, get the best of both worlds by converting existing policies to paid-up policies and having your wife use the premium money to take out new policies.

In transferring policies on your life to new owners, these points should be considered—

(1) If the owner dies before you, the then value of the policies will be taxable in his or her estate. This may be a point for giving the policies to your children or to a trust rather than to your wife.

(2) If you continue to make the premium payments, each payment will be treated as a gift to the owner. If your wife or children are the owners, this gift may be protected from gift tax by the $3,000 annual exclusion for each donee, which is doubled if the wife joins in the gift. If the policy is owned by a trust (other than a § 2503(c) trust for a minor), the payment of premiums will be a gift of a future interest, the

annual exclusion will not be available, and after consuming the $30,000 lifetime exemption ($60,000 for husband and wife), gift tax liability will be incurred with each premium payment.

GIFTS OF LIFE INSURANCE
PREMIUMS AFTER ASSIGNMENT

Insurance proceeds may still be included in your taxable estate even though the transfer was not "in contemplation of death" (within three years of your death) where you continue to pay premiums within three years prior to your death. The Treasury says that the portion of the proceeds purchased with these premiums is taxable in your estate. Therefore, for example, if you paid premiums of $1,500 during the three years prior to your death and the total premiums paid during the lifetime of the policy amounted to $6,000, 25 per cent of the proceeds ($1500/$6000) would be includable in your estate.

The government may be wrong in this position. It can be argued that the transfer of the policy either is or is not "in contemplation of death"; and since Congress has eliminated the premium-payment test, the subsequent payment of premiums by you should not in itself cause any part of the proceeds of a transfer that is not in contemplation of death to be includable in your estate. Only the amount of premiums paid in the three years prior to death should be included in your estate.

Still, to avoid this unsettled question it is advisable to have the new owner of a transferred insurance policy pay future premiums. If he or she doesn't have the cash, it is better to make a gift of the money and leave it to the discretion of the donee to pay the premiums than for the donor to pay the premiums directly.

WHO SHOULD GET THE PROCEEDS?

These are the points for you to consider—

(1) Are the proceeds likely to be taxed soon in the estate of the beneficiary? This argues for making the proceeds payable to your children rather than to your wife. If the proceeds are payable to a trust, your wife and children can get the income, and estate tax can be avoided over two generations.

(2) What assurance is there that the proceeds will be available to provide liquidity needed by your estate? Possibly your wife and children will have a sufficient interest in the estate or can otherwise be counted on to feed the proceeds back into the estate by loan or by the purchase of assets.

There are only two ways to make sure that the proceeds will be made available to your estate—

(1) Make the proceeds payable to your estate. This is bad, because it gets back into an estate tax.

(2) Make the proceeds payable to a trust, that is empowered to buy assets from or lend money to the estate.

TWO PITFALLS TO WATCH CLOSELY

Here are two possible surprises that require the closest attention—

(1) If you have a policy in which your children are named as beneficiaries and you transfer that policy to your wife, you'll succeed in removing the proceeds from your estate at the cost of a possible gift tax. But, on your death, the proceeds will be deemed to have been received by your children as a taxable gift from your wife. (This is in addition to any gift tax you may have paid on the transfer of the policy to your wife.) *Reason:* During your life, while she had incidents of ownership, she had the power to change the beneficiaries. Having refrained from changing the beneficiaries, she is

deemed to have made the gift at the last instant before she could no longer change the beneficiaries, that is, the last instant before her death.

To avoid this type of result, consider transferring the policy to an irrevocable trust, naming the trust the beneficiary of the insurance and the children as beneficiaries of the trust. If you do this, there are two possibilities open to you. You can either—

(a) Fund the trust so that it has income to pay the premiums. Any taxable gift will arise *only* on the transfer to the trust and that will be confined to the assets transferred to fund the trust.

(b) Pay the annual premiums to the trust. Here, your gift tax will be confined to the premiums, which will usually be preferable to having it applied to the proceeds.

In either case, there will be tax savings.

(2) The second possible surprise can distort the distribution plan of the entire estate. More and more insurance is being financed by borrowed money. If your insurance has been used as collateral for a loan on which you are personally liable, and the lender repays himself out of the insurance proceeds, your beneficiary may be able to make the balance of the estate pay him the amount of the loan. This can inadvertently give the beneficiary of bank-loan insurance not the net value of the insurance, but its gross value at the expense of other beneficiaries of your estate. This result is not likely to occur where your insurance company and not a bank has made the loan. The law varies from state to state. It is important then, when you borrow on an insurance policy, that the loan instrument and your will spell out your intent as to whether the loan is to be paid by the policy proceeds only or by the entire estate. A general clause in your will should provide for these situations.

HOW THE INSURANCE PROCEEDS SHOULD BE PAID

Insurance proceeds may be paid outright to the beneficiary or under one of the optional modes of settlement (held by the insurance company at interest with withdrawal rights or payable in installments in a fixed amount or over a fixed number of years or for life).

Life insurance proceeds can be paid to:

(a) your estate (your executor), or

(b) natural persons, or

(c) trustee of a living trust created by you during your lifetime, or

(d) trustee of a trust created in your will.

Making the proceeds payable to your executor is useful if the proceeds are intended to be used to cover debts, funeral expenses, taxes, and administration expenses. Such a designation, however, will subject the proceeds to probate, state and federal death taxes, and creditor's claims. A way to avoid this and still obtain liquidity to pay administration expenses and death taxes is to name your wife as beneficiary. Your wife can provide your estate with liquidity by lending the cash proceeds to your estate or by purchasing estate assets.

Where you think that your wife cannot be counted on to use the money to meet estate costs, you can assure this result by using a trust. Designate the trustee as beneficiary and have him lend the money or purchase assets.

Still, you will be following the most common course by naming your wife the beneficiary. Generally, the wife is named primary beneficiary, with children as contingent beneficiaries. This designation results in the proceeds avoiding probate and state inheritance taxes. The proceeds will also be excluded from your Federal estate if you relinquish all incidents of ownership in the policy.

The designation may read: "Mary Jones, wife of the insured, if living at the time of the death of the insured, otherwise to the children of the insured, equally, or to the survivor of them, as may be living at the death of the insured."

If you anticipate having the beneficiary use the proceeds to provide liquidity for your estate, make sure that the proceeds are payable in cash or payable on an interest option with privilege of withdrawal at any time. Otherwise, the money will be tied up with the insurance company.

When leaving insurance proceeds to minors, a legal guardian must be appointed to receive the proceeds on their behalf. Generally, an insurance company will not allow the proceeds to be received directly by the child unless he is at least 18 years of age. If you want the children to receive the proceeds in installments, you have to elect this option yourself in advance, since the guardian will probably not have the right to select one of the installment options for the minor.

Designating children as beneficiary by specific names must be carefully considered. Assume the clause designates, "James, William, and Helen, children of the insured" as beneficiaries. A child born after the designation would be excluded from the benefits of the policy unless the insured changed the designation after the child was born, which is frequently not done.

The safer designation is: "Children of the insured, including James, William, and Helen." This protects the after-born child, even though the insured neglects to revise the designation after the birth of the child. An alternative approach is: "James, William, and Helen, children of the insured and any children of the insured hereafter born or legally adopted."

Using the phrase, "children born of the marriage of the

insured and his said wife" presents a hazard because it fails to cover children born from either a subsequent or a previous marriage of the insured. This provision also excludes adopted children. The simple clause "children of the insured" would overcome this possible pitfall, but be careful where, as we indicated earlier, you specify the names of the children.

Where you wish to leave a portion of the proceeds to the children of a deceased child, you should specifically indicate this in the policy, as follows: "The children of a deceased child shall receive his (or her) parent's share of the proceeds."

When a daughter is named as beneficiary, review your policies when she marries. By changing the beneficiary designation to her full married name, you remove all doubts as to her identification, and speedy payment of the proceeds will be made without the necessity of affidavits or any other legal proof of her identity.

Designating stepchildren or children adopted without formal adoption proceedings should be done by specifically naming them. Adopted children, the courts have held, come within the phrase "the children of the insured." But adoption proceedings sometimes take months or even years. Until the proceedings are completed, such children might not be considered within the designation "children of the insured." Therefore, to play it safe, it is better in those circumstances to name the child specifically so that your intention will be clearly indicated.

NAMING A TRUST AS BENEFICIARY

Using a trust as beneficiary offers greater flexibility in investment management and in application of the proceeds to meet family needs. These are the advantages of payment to a trust:

(1) The trust may be a method of eliminating the trouble and expense of a guardian in the case of minor beneficiaries. The beneficiary clauses of the life insurance trust serve the same purposes as the special settlement provisions that are often attached to life insurance policies.

(2) The trust makes possible the elimination of successive transfer taxes in those instances where life estates in the trust income are given to elderly beneficiaries, with gifts of the principal to others at the death of such beneficiaries.

(3) Subject to statutory limitations in each state, income may be accumulated by the trustee until the beneficiary reaches a certain age, when the principal is to be turned over to the beneficiary. It is important to note that in many states accumulations are permissible only during the minority of the beneficiary.

(4) A great number of contingencies can be provided for in the directions to the trustee concerning distribution of income and principal of the trust.

(5) It is possible to grant the trustee discretion in the solution of many problems that the insurance company could not handle itself. This includes the selection of a member of the class of beneficiaries on the basis of need or by any other discretionary yardstick.

(6) Restrictions and limitations on the use and enjoyment of the property by the beneficiary may be incorporated in the trust. Such restrictions would not be possible with the ordinary insurance options.

(7) Broad discretion in the selection of investments can be placed in the trustee's hands. Thus, with a capable trustee, it is possible that income realized through investments of trust funds may be greater than that guaranteed by the insurance company in the policy options—but without the guarantees.

(8) A life insurance trust can, by appropriate instructions to the trustees, provide estate liquidity for estate tax purposes and still keep important income-producing assets in the family.

HOW TO SET UP A LIFE INSURANCE TRUST

The life insurance trust is a happy wedding of two of the most useful estate planning tools. It is a trust set up during your lifetime, which, among other provisions, provides that the trustee is to receive and administer insurance proceeds that become payable at your death. You may also have other assets pouring over into this trust (from your will, from employee benefit plans, etc.) to make for a uniform administration and management of the bulk of your property.

An insurance trust may be *revocable* or *irrevocable*. It may be *funded* or *unfunded*. This simplest and most often used arrangement is the *revocable unfunded life insurance trust*.

REVOCABLE TRUST,

A typical arrangement, once the trust agreement has been executed, is for the life insurance proceeds to be made payable to the trustee. The policies are usually deposited with the trustee. But you are still the owner of the policies. Not only can you make whatever changes you wish in the trust (including cancelling it altogether), but you also retain all rights in the policies and can drop them or make any other changes you see fit. Since the trust is nonfunded, you continue to pay the premiums.

Assuming you don't revoke the trust, upon your death, the trustee will collect the proceeds, invest them, pay the trust's net income to the trust's income beneficiary, and then eventually pay the principal to the remainder beneficiaries.

The proceeds escape probate but not Federal estate tax, except to the extent that they qualify for the marital deduction.

Under a variation of this basic revocable trust arrangement, you actually assign the policies to the trustee (this may be required in some states). But the assignment of the policies to the trustee is a mere formality since you can always have the policies reassigned to you should you choose to revoke the trust.

You may or may not want the insurance proceeds in trust to qualify for the marital deduction. If you have sufficient assets other than the life insurance to pass to your wife so as to qualify for the marital deduction, you wouldn't need the insurance trust to qualify since it would be wasted here. So what you would do is to set up the trust for the life of your wife with remainder over to your children or with your wife having a limited power to distribute the proceeds among your children. Where, on the other hand, you do want these insurance proceeds to qualify for the marital deduction, this can be done easily by including appropriate provisions in the trust instrument to meet the requirements. (See page 97.)

IRREVOCABLE TRUST

Unlike the revocable life insurance trust, the irrevocable life insurance trust does have some significant income and estate tax benefits in addition to the benefit of avoiding probate and state inheritance taxes. The big drawback, however, is that you lose complete control of the policy during your lifetime. Another disadvantage is that you will be subject to gift taxes to the extent of the value of the policy and any subsequent premiums you might pay.

The typical life insurance trust situation involves a man

(the insured), his wife, and his children. In such a case, estate tax savings at the wife's death, following that of her husband, can be important.

An irrevocable life insurance trust may be designed so as to avoid inclusion of any portion of the insurance proceeds in either the husband's estate or the wife's estate for Federal estate tax purposes. This is done by having the trust give the wife a life income with the trust property passing on to the children or other beneficiaries after the wife's death. But you can add a good deal more flexibility to the package without necessarily sacrificing any estate tax savings. For example, the trustee can be given a discretionary power to use principal for the wife's benefit. And with but little estate tax effect, if any, the wife herself could be given a limited power to withdraw principal from the trust.

And she may also have a limited, but not general, power of appointment.

For example, in lieu of the trust instrument directing that the insurance proceeds held by the trust should go to the children when the wife dies, it could direct that they be allocated among those of the children and in such proportions as the wife determines—i.e., appoints. This limited power of appointment will not cause the trust property to be included in her estate under the tax law. (But note that she can't appoint just anyone; the power is limited to one, some, or all of her children.) And yet, as a practical matter, since she would normally be appointing to her children pretty much in any event, you do have the equivalent of a general power of appointment.

Where enough of the husband's noninsurance property (e.g., the home, bank deposits, some jointly owned securities, specific property left under his will, etc.) is going to pass to the wife in a manner that qualifies for the maximum marital deduction, then the same "second-death" estate tax saving arrangement shown above in connection with the irrevocable trust can be worked out with the revocable life insurance trust as well.

By giving away all of your "incidents of ownership" in an insurance policy, you can remove the proceeds from your taxable estate even though you may continue to pay the premiums. Transfer to a *revocable* trust won't do the trick; but a transfer of all incidents of ownership to the trustee of an *irrevocable* trust will.

In order for the irrevocable life insurance trust to have an income-tax effect during your life, the trust must be funded. The reason is simple: An unfunded trust has no income during your lifetime. Only a funded trust can have income.

It is possible to get income-tax savings with an irrevocable trust if the trustee uses trust income to pay for insurance on your (grantor) life. Such income is not taxable to you provided the beneficiary has the right under the trust instrument to approve or consent to the payment.

The creation of an irrevocable life insurance trust, whether funded or unfunded, constitutes a gift. So the estate tax savings (and income-tax savings, in the case of certain funded insurance trusts) do not come cost free. However, the method of valuation of the gift of insurance still affords quite a sizable tax advantage. This is because the gift tax is computed on the value of the policy on the date of the gift and not at its increased value at the death of the insured.

HOW A REVOCABLE LIFE INSURANCE TRUST COMPARES WITH A TRUST SET UP IN YOUR WILL

Since a revocable life insurance trust set up during your life is virtually the equivalent of making life insurance proceeds payable to a trust created in your will to take effect at death, why should we choose the revocable trust route? The answer is that there are significant differences between these arrangements. The differences depend on the varying state laws and to a lesser degree in some cases on the administrative policy of the life insurance companies. On the state law front, inquiry should be directed to the question of whether proceeds can be made payable directly to a trustee named in your will or must be payable in the first instance to your estate, then to be transmitted to the trustee named in the will, and what significance this distinction has. Here are some of the general distinctions between the will and a living trust approach:

(1) *Probate expenses*—Since the will-created trust derives its existence from the will, whereas the living trust does not, the chances are that probate expenses incurred under the will-created trust will be greater than the trustee fees and other expenses incurred with a living trust. In addition, while legal expenses will usually be incurred in either vehicle, the chances are that the lower costs will be incurred with the living revocable trust.

(2) *Court supervision*—Following the death of the insured, the chances that continuing court supervision of the trust (especially where minor beneficiaries are concerned) will be required, and at some indirect cost to the beneficiaries, are much greater in connection with the will-created or testamentary trust than with the living trust.

(3) *Exemption of insurance proceeds from state death tax*—Most of the state death tax statutes grant at least partial exemptions for life insurance proceeds payable to named beneficiaries, as distinguished from proceeds payable to the insured's estate. While each state's laws, both the statutory and case law, will have to be looked into, there is considerably

greater likelihood that the proceeds will be deemed to be paid to named beneficiaries rather than to the estate when they are paid to the trustee of a living trust than when they are paid to a testamentary trustee.

(4) *Creditor's claims*—Where the insurance proceeds are payable directly to the estate, under local state law, they may not be exempt from claims of creditors of the insured.

(5) *Whose law is to govern the trust?*—Whether for reasons of beneficiary convenience or perhaps because of more liberal trust laws in one state than in another, you may prefer that your trust be governed by the laws of some state other than where you live, perhaps even with an out-of-state trustee. This can be accomplished with a living trust. It is much more difficult, if not altogether impossible, to achieve either of these arrangements via the testamentary trust.

(6)*Administrative practice of insurance companies*—Despite the fact that state law in a given case may permit the designation of a testamentary trustee as beneficiary of insurance proceeds, it is entirely possible that an insurance company may refuse to go along with this—or may set up serious obstacles. On the other hand, insurance companies as a rule will let you designate the trustee of a living trust (even though it is a revocable trust) as your beneficiary.

(7) *Availability of proceeds*—When you make insurance proceeds payable to a trustee of a living trust, there is usually little or no delay (other than the time required to produce a death certificate) in having the proceeds paid to the trustee. On the other hand, if the proceeds are payable to the estate, there may be delay until the executor actually sets up the trust. And even if the proceeds are payable directly to a testamentary trustee, there will at least be some delay during the period required to probate the will and qualify the trustee.

In evaluating the use of a living trust, all its advantages should be weighed against the fact that time, effort, and expenses are involved in creating and maintaining it during the lifetime of the insured.

If you choose the revocable trust, you might consider funding the trust with income-producing property, transferring it along with the policy to the trust. Although you are still taxed on the income earned by the property, you are given a preview of how your trustee will function. And if you are not satisfied, you'll have the opportunity to make a change. With an unfunded trust you will not be able to put the trustee to the test since he merely holds the policy.

HOW A FUNDED LIFE INSURANCE TRUST CAN CARRY MORE INSURANCE

The funded life insurance trust is on in which income-producing property is transferred to a trust, and the trust is either given or directed to take out an insurance policy that may be made payable to the trust or to named beneficiaries.

If the trust carries insurance on your life and you set it up, the income of the trust will be taxed to you. But if you create a trust and direct that the income be used to carry insurance on the life of your wife or your son, the trust income will be taxed to the trust. This offers an important opportunity to make your investment income more valuable and carry more insurance on another person's life than it would carry if it were taxed to you.

This method affords income-tax savings by transferring top-bracket income to another taxable entity—a trust. This is particularly effective in building family security where investment income is received on top of salary or business income. If a father has adequate security he saves future estate tax and expands family income by the transfer of income-producing property to a trust.

Here is an approximation of how much insurance can be bought by a married individual filing a joint return with a tax savings from the transfer of $1,000 of investment income to a trust:

SHIFTING $1,000 OF INCOME TO TRUST

Gross Income	Tax Saving	Ordinary life at age 30	40	50
$10,000	$ 60	$ 3,915	$ 2,634	$ 1,764
20,000	150	9,627	6,584	4,424
30,000	230	14,762	10,096	6,784
40,000	320	20,544	14,048	9,440
50,000	370	23,754	16,243	10,915
60,000	400	25,680	17,560	11,800

A FUNDED TRUST ON HUSBAND OR WIFE

When a wife has income-producing property, a good use that can frequently be made of the income is to shift the income-producing property to a trust and have it used to carry insurance on the husband's life. The wife's own income is usually taxed in the same high tax bracket as the husband with his earned income and his own investment income. By shifting the wife's investment income to a trust, it is taxed at lower rates and can carry a lot more insurance than the husband's can with the same amount of pretax investment income. This arrangement takes the burden of adequate insurance off the husband's after-tax dollars.

Or the husband may transfer some of his investment assets to a trust to make them more effective by carrying insurance on his wife's life. This makes sense in many cases where the wife's earlier death, eliminating the estate tax marital deduction, would substantially increase the tax cost of passing the husband's estate to his children. The difference between the net estate tax, with and without the marital deduction, represents a financial risk that can well be covered by a funded life insurance trust carrying insurance on a wife.

Here is how the mathematics of a husband-wife funded trust work out: Mr. and Mrs. Reilly, Mrs. Reilly having an independent source of income, are in the 50 per cent joint income-tax bracket. The net taxable estate of Mr. Reilly (after allowing for 50 per cent of marital deduction) would be approximately $1,000,000. A funded life insurance trust, established with $100,000 of Mrs. Reilly's stock portfolio yielding 4 per cent, taking out insurance on the life of Mr. Reilly, would project the following figures at age 50:

	No Trust— Insurance Owned by Mrs. Reilly	Funded Trust
Before-tax income on $100,000	$ 4,000	$ 4,000
After-tax income on $100,000	2,000	3,350
Insurance buyable (whole-life, nonpar, at age 50)	59,000	99,000

So, the establishment of an irrevocable trust by Mrs. Reilly with $100,000 of her own property will provide enough additional after-tax return to purchase $40,000 more insurance on Mr. Reilly's life than she could buy with the after-tax income on the same $100,000 if she does not set up the trust.

HOW TO TIE IN YOUR INSURANCE WITH YOUR WILL

To plan your estate properly, you should integrate your insurance program with the provisions of your will. Here are some important steps that you might take:

(1) *Authority to Buy Annuity:* (a) You may want a specified amount of income to be paid for life to the beneficiary of a trust created under your will. The will may provide for a specified amount to be paid out of income and principal, if necessary. Under these circumstances, your will should authorize the trustee at his discretion to buy an annuity to guarantee these payments. (b) Similarly, where your executor is directed to pay a specific bequest to an employee or relative, you should consider whether or not the requirements and the situation of that employee or relative might not better be served by authorizing the executor to invest the amount of the legacy in an annuity for that person.

(2) *Wasting Asset - Wife Insurance:* The principal asset of a trust created by your will may be a wasting one, so that after payment of income is made to the beneficiary, say your wife, there will be little or nothing left for the children. In these circumstances, you might authorize the trustee to guarantee some remainder capital for the children by directing him to invest some of the income in a life insurance policy on the life of the beneficiary. When the beneficiary dies, the insurance proceeds can then be used to provide something for the children or other beneficiaries.

(3) *Death Taxes:* The arrangement and the value of an insurance estate may depend on what the will says about the payment of estate taxes. Death taxes may be paid out of a residuary estate or be apportioned against all items of property making up the estate, including the insurance proceeds. Where the settlement options are favorable, you should direct that the death taxes shall *not* be paid out of the insurance proceeds.

(4) *Insurance on Lives of Wife and Children:* Where you have purchased insurance on the life of your children,

the source of premium payments for these policies will be cut off at death. Should your will authorize the executor to pay up or convert such policies to paid-up insurance? If you own a life insurance policy on the life of your wife, what disposition should be made of the policy and what arrangement should be made for payment of premiums during the period the policy is part of an estate in administration? What authority should you give your executor to make a premium loan, elect paid-up insurance, or surrender the policy?

(5) *Option Settlements:* Insurance option settlement arrangements should be integrated with arrangements in the will for the distribution of income out of trusts created under your will and with the final distribution of capital from your estate.

(6) *Insurance Proceeds and Marital Deduction:* The arrangements with respect to whether or not the insurance proceeds will qualify for the marital deduction must be integrated with similar arrangements with respect to other property as provided in your will.

(7) *Business Continuation:* If there is insurance in connection with a buy-and-sell agreement or a plan for the retirement of stock, it is essential to see that the will contains coordinated provisions authorizing the executor and/or trustees to carry on the business or to continue to hold stock or business interests as estate or trust investments, or it may require a specific direction to liquidate the business.

(8) *Guardianship of Child Insurance Beneficiaries:* Provisions for payment of life insurance proceeds to children as contingent beneficiaries should be properly integrated with provisions for guardianship or other arrangements for the payment of income and principal for the account of children during their minority.

(9) *Power of Spouse Over Proceeds:* Where insurance is included among your estate assets subject to the marital deduction, and where contingent beneficiaries are named in the life insurance policy, the beneficiary clause in the policy should contain appropriate language giving the spouse the power to withdraw the proceeds or appoint to her estate. This power is necessary to have the proceeds qualify for the marital deduction.

(10) *Annuity for Spouse:* If your will *directs* the conversion of estate assets into cash for the purchase of an annuity merely for the life of your surviving spouse, the proceeds will not qualify for the marital deduction. She has to have the power, as noted in (9), to withdraw the proceeds or appoint them to her estate or to someone else.

(11) *Power of Trustee in Insurance Trust:* In an insurance trust, you should give the trustee discretion and power to select settlement options that will qualify the trust for the marital deduction.

(12) *Installment or Life Income Options for Spouse:* You should consider having insurance proceeds distributed to your spouse under installments or life income options. This is a method of utilizing the marital deduction, minimizing or eliminating tax on your spouse's death and having her realize up to $1000 of "interest" payouts, income-tax free.

(13) *Remainder to Charity:* You should consider maximizing the income available to your wife by giving a remainder interest to charity after her death.

(14) *Mortgage Cancellation Insurance:* Beneficiary arrangements of "mortgage cancellation insurance" should be set up so that your wife is given a free choice whether or not to pay off the mortgage.

CHAPTER XII

SHOULD YOU MAKE FAMILY GIFTS

Should you make family gifts? The answer is NO, unless you're confident you'll never need what you give away. If you have that confidence, read on.

The most direct and effective method of reducing your taxable estate is by making gifts during your lifetime to those who would be the beneficiaries under your will. These gifts may be made tax free if kept within the gift tax exemptions and exclusions. A program of lifetime gifts, when planned and carried on over a period of years, may produce substantial savings in taxes. Even when a lifetime gift exceeds the exemption and annual exclusions so that a gift tax is payable, ultimate tax savings result from these four factors.

(1) The gift tax rates are only three-quarters of the estate tax rates.

(2) The gift property is taken from the donor's top estate tax brackets and transferred to the bottom gift tax brackets.

(3) The estate tax is imposed not only on the property actually transferred to heirs, but also on the property used to pay the estate tax. When $100,000 is passed by bequest in your will and that segment of the estate is subject to a 25 per cent tax rate, the person to whom the bequest is made receives only $75,000. Nevertheless, the estate tax is levied on $100,000. On the other hand, when a lifetime gift of $75,000 is made, the gift tax applies only to the net amount received by the donee.

(4) When property is transferred from one member of a family to another, whether by gift or for value, we are ac-

complishing not only the elimination of the property from the estate of the transferor, but are also keeping out future appreciation from his estate and future increases in income from his income-tax return. The cummulative effect can be great.

The prospective death tax savings to be achieved by a lifetime gift may not be as powerful a motivating force as the prospect of immediate income-tax savings. These income-tax savings, achieved for the family group when income-producing property is transferred to your children outright or in trust or when your business is converted to a family partnership, can accumulate over the years to a substantial amount of capital, which will also, of course, be outside your taxable estate.

A negative factor to be considered is the accumulated capital value of the loss of income to you that results from your payment of the gift tax. If, for example, you make a large enough gift to call for the payment of $50,000 gift tax, you must weigh against the anticipated estate tax savings and any annual income-tax savings that may result from shifting the income from the gift property into lower surtax brackets: your personal loss of the income on $50,000 of gift tax money that will no longer be working for you and the capital that income might generate and accumulate over your life expectancy.

You also must be satisfied that your donees will handle their gifts wisely if you want to make the gifts outright. Otherwise, you should protect the property by using a trust. This is particularly true in the case of a gift of shares in a family corporation. Irresponsible voters of a minority stock interest in a closed corporation can find ways to interfere with management of the business or block a sale, reorganization, or liquidation.

ESTATE TAX SAVINGS IN GIFTS

Assuming you can spare the capital, the estate tax saved by making lifetime gifts is substantial. The following table shows the tax savings by gifts of 25 per cent and 50 per cent of the husband's estate. It is assumed that the gifts are made in a lump sum to two children. It is also assumed that the gifts are joint gifts and that no previous gifts have been made.

Size of Adjusted Gross Estate	Savings With No Marital Deduction Gift of		Savings With Full Marital Deduction Gift of	
	25%	50%	25%	50%
$ 100,000	$ 3,750	$ 4,800	$ 0	$ 0
200,000	14,800	26,744	3,750	3,390
300,000	22,452	39,810	10,215	10,301
400,000	30,813	50,649	13,587	13,404
500,000	37,439	60,299	15,549	13,824
600,000	44,488	70,855	16,609	12,679
700,000	52,678	82,980	17,647	11,804
800,000	59,645	94,502	18,259	10,927
900,000	66,783	107,652	18,209	9,865
1,000,000	74,120	121,002	17,799	8,802
2,000,000	175,437	295,674	23,361	7,933
5,000,000	664,079	1,141,643	93,261	72,602
10,000,000	1,712,278	3,045,830	338,907	339,299

INCOME-TAX SAVINGS IN GIFTS

It is very expensive for a person in a high tax bracket to give money to another member of the family. If, for example, a man in the 70 per cent tax bracket gives his mother $200 a month, each payment costs him $667 in the sense that he must earn that much or have property yielding that much to have left after taxes the $200 with which to make a payment. On the other hand, a gift of property that will throw off an equivalent amount of after-tax income can result in a substantial reduction or even complete elimination of the tax bite, depending on the donee's tax bracket. For example, although a $2,000 yearly allowance is tax free to the dependent, it is costly to the estate owner. Here is a comparison of the income cost of the yearly gift with that of a gift of property yielding $2,200 annually, the amount necessary to net $2,000 assuming a $200 income tax liability to the donee.

Donor's Effective Tax Rate	Income Required to Net $2,000 After Taxes	Income from Transferred Property	Income Retained by Donor	Donor's After-Tax Income Saving
30%	$2,857	$2,200	$ 657	$ 460
40%	3,333	2,200	1,133	680
50%	4,000	2,200	1,800	900
60%	5,000	2,200	2,800	1,120
70%	6,667	2,200	4,467	1,340

WHAT GIFTS COST

Each person has a $30,000 lifetime exemption that can be doubled if the gift is reported as being made by the husband and wife together. In addition, each year a $3,000 additional exemption may be taken on account of each person to whom gifts are made. Up to $6,000 can be claimed by the donor and his spouse even though only one owns the gift property. In addition, the Code permits a marital deduction on half the amount of a gift from one spouse to the other. Thus, the *cost of a gift* will vary, depending on whether it is made by a single person, by a married person to his spouse, or by a married person to someone else.

The table below shows the cost of a gift assuming full $30,-000 lifetime gift exemptions. Before using the table, subtract the $3,000 annual exclusion ($6,000 for gifts in which spouse joins). For example, the tax on a $90,000 gift to a spouse would be computed as shown on the next page.

$90,000 gift less $3,000 annual exclusion	$87,000
Tax on $80,000 gift to spouse from table	375
Tax on ½ the excess of $7,000 at 8¼%	288.75
	$ 663.75

Example of use of this table:

How much gift tax is due on a gift to a wife of $90,000 where the husband still has his full $30,000 lifetime exemption?

$90,000 gift less $3,000 annual exclusion	$87,000
Tax on $80,000 gift to spouse from table	$375
Tax on 1/2 the excess of $7,000 at 8-1/4%	289
Total gift tax	$664

Note: The $3,000 annual exclusion ($6,000 for gift in which spouse joins) mush be deducted before using this table. Table utilizes $30,000 ($60,000) lifetime exemption.

Amount of Gift Exceeds	Tax on Ordinary Gifts	Rate on Excess Amount	Tax on Gift to Spouse	Tax on Gift in Which Spouse Joins	Rate on 1/2 Excess Amount	Saving When Spouse Joins
$ 30,000	$	2 1/4%	$	$	%	$
35,000	112	5 1/4				112
40,000	375	8 1/4				375
50,000	1,200	10 1/2				1,200
60,000	2,250	13 1/2			2 1/4	2,250
65,000	2,925	13 1/2	56	112	2 1/4	2,813
70,000	3,600	16 1/2	112	225	5 1/4	3,375
80,000	5,250	18 3/4	375	750	8 1/4	4,500
90,000	7,125	21	787	1,575	8 1/4	5,550
100,000	9,225	21	1,200	2,400	10 1/2	6,825
120,000	13,425	21	2,250	4,500	13 1/2	8,925
130,000	15,525	22 1/2	2,925	5,850	13 1/2	9,675
140,000	17,775	22 1/2	3,600	7,200	16 1/2	10,575
150,000	20,025	22 1/2	4,425	8,850	16 1/2	11,175
160,000	22,275	22 1/2	5,250	10,500	18 3/4	11,775
180,000	26,775	22 1/2	7,125	14,250	21	12,525
200,000	31,275	22 1/2	9,225	18,450	21	12,825
250,000	42,525	22 1/2	14,475	28,950	21	13,575

WHAT TO GIVE

In selecting property to use in making family gifts, these are your major considerations:

1. Property for which you are not likely to have any need.

Insurance on your life is likely to rank high in this respect. Stock that does not disturb control in a family corporation may meet this specification, but you should reflect that there are such things as stockholders' derivative actions and sales and mergers in which ownership of less than 100 per cent of the stock can be an embarrassment.

2. Property with a low value for gift tax purposes and a high value for estate tax purposes. Life insurance valued at cash or terminal reserve value for gift purposes and face value for estate tax purposes fit this specification. So do stock and land that has not yet attained its full value. But it is painful to waste gift tax and gift exemptions on overvalued property that then goes down where it belongs.

3. Assets not likely to be sold are good for gift purposes because the loss of the higher basis brought about by death is not consequential. Don't make gifts of assets that cost little and have high value; it is better to hold them and let the estate tax save the capital gains tax. If you give these assets to your children during your life, they also get a built-in capital gains tax liability.

4. Don't make gifts of exhausting assets or assets that have lost value. You minimize estate tax savings and give up possible income-tax benefit from realizing losses in value.

TIMING THE GIFT.

The assets factor entering into our gift-making strategy is that of timing. Consider the following:

(1) *Market Fluctuations.* In timing gifts, a strategy frequently overlooked is the gift of growth type property when it is in one of its secondary declines. For example, during the market dips in 1946, 1950, 1954, 1957, 1962, and 1966, there were many good growth stocks, including some so-called blue

chips, which dropped as much as 50 per cent or more below their highs for the year. Timing a gift program to take advantage of temporary setbacks in the price of stocks and other property affords a tremendous opportunity to maximize gifts with a minimum of gift tax liability.

(2) *Avoiding Contemplation of Death Problem.* Gifts should be timed to coincide with important occasions in the donee's life, such as the donee's birthday, anniversary, Christmas, purchase of a new home, starting a new business, and so on. The reason for this strategy is to substantiate the lifetime motive of the gift.

(3) *Deathbed Gifts.* Although a gift in contemplation of death does not remove the value of the gift from the donor's taxable estate, the estate will be reduced by the amount of the gift taxes paid. Since the gift tax is allowed as a credit against the estate tax, there is an overall estate tax savings on the transaction. Obviously, this tax ploy isn't for everyone. But if you are in the fortunate position of having several million dollars, a deathbed gift can result in a fairly respectable tax saving.

(4) *Year-End Gift Strategy.* Before each year ends, the gift situation should be reviewed. Since there is a $3,000 ($6,000 on joint gifts with spouse) exclusion on gifts to each donee, a gift of that amount before the end of the year is a must in any gift program.

If donor hasn't used up his gift exclusion limit and doesn't before the end of the year, he just loses the exclusion forever. On the other hand, there are situations when it is better to postpone the gift to the next year or spread it over two years. Where the contemplated gift is substantially enough so that there will be a tax owing even after the application of the available exclusions and exemptions, then another very important, though often overlooked, consideration enters into the picture: that is, does it make sense to lay out the gift tax money this coming April 15? Or would it be better to postpone the gift until the first of the year and have the gift tax money in the donor's pocket until April 15 of the following year?

CHAPTER XIII

SHOULD YOU SET UP TRUSTS NOW

You may want to establish a trust now for one of three main purposes:

1. To hold the bulk of your property in a revocable trust, which will become the medium of holding and distributing your property for your family. We call this the living, or revocable, trust and dealt with it in Chapter IX.

2. To serve as a means of collecting assets that will become available at your death free of estate taxes if not payable to your estate and assets that pass to the trust under the terms of your will. We call this a naked or pourover trust. It may be set up revocably or irrevocably and usually includes assets having little present value.

3. To keep assets out of your estate, to keep investment income out of your income-tax return, to protect you and your family from folly, or to serve other family purposes. This kind of family trust is set up irrevocably and with assets having more substantial value than those used in the naked trust. Both can be used for pourover purposes.

POUROVER OF ASSETS FROM A WILL TO A LIVING TRUST

A "pourover" trust is one that exists outside the will, is independent of the will, and serves as a receptacle for property that is given it by the will.

The basic advantages this device offers you are these—

(1) All provisions for the ultimate disposition of your

property appear in the living trust—it is not necessary to repeat the terms of the pourover trust in your will.

(2) The provisions of the living trust need not be made public as must the provisions of your will.

(3) Since all the "poured over" assets will be administered under the living trust, many of the costs and conveniences involved in probate administration will be avoided.

(4) You have a chance to see your representative, as trustee, manage a segment of your estate before death makes the arrangement irrevocable.

Any person with an assortment of assets, those he owns outright and those that come to him from the corporation that employs him, has a problem of coordinating them into a coherent pattern and focusing them on his family objectives. One effective method of accomplishing this is to create an inter vivos or living trust and name it beneficiary in his will, in the beneficiary designations he gives to his insurance companies, and those he gives to his employer to apply to pension, profit-sharing, stock bonus, and other deferred compensation rights. Thus, by the terms of this trust he can control how all these assets are to be accumulated, distributed, and used for his family's benefit. He cannot give a lot of complicated directions to his corporate employer to govern the distribution of group insurance proceeds, pension and profit-sharing death benefits, or deferred compensation payments. He could direct that these payments be made to his estate and then, by his will, provide that his executors and testamentary trustees follow his complicated directions. However, if he does this, with the estate as beneficiary, he loses the estate tax exemption available for pension and profit-sharing death benefits arising from the employer's contributions when these are made payable to a named beneficiary.

If he creates a pourover trust during his lifetime and

names it the beneficiary of these death benefits, he can preserve his death tax exemption. In fact, the use of the pourover trust can avoid the second tax, which would be payable on the death of an individual named as beneficiary. If an executive simply directs his company to make his wife the beneficiary of its contribution to the death benefit, this portion will go to the wife free of estate tax. However, on her subsequent death they will fall subject to estate tax. On the other hand, if the executive creates a lifetime trust—which can be revocable until his death—names it the beneficiary to receive pension and profit-sharing death benefits, and provides that trust income shall be distributed to his wife for life with the principal going to the children on her death, he will have avoided the estate tax at the death of his wife as well as that on his own death.

In addition, by providing for a lump-sum distribution of all pension or profit-sharing benefits to a trust, we get capital gain rates the same as for lump-sum distribution to a wife. Many men would prefer not to have their wives come into outright possession of a large sum; they prefer to keep the money tied up under professional management.

A corporate executive will have an additional problem as to certain corporate payments that can't be received as capital gain. Under a deferred compensation contract or a deferred stock bonus, postdeath payments made by his corporate employer are fully taxable as ordinary income when received. If these payments are made to a single entity, especially where income-splitting is no longer available, the value of these payments as future capital is sharply diminished by the income-tax liability that attaches to them when received. To avoid or minimize this, he can provide that these payments are to be divided equally among more than one trust, to be treated as trust capital when received. There will still be an income tax payable by the trusts on receipt, but it will not be necessary to treat this money as distributable trust income. As a result, the income tax will be at the rates applicable to the trusts. By spreading the payments, the income-tax liability may be held down so that there is more permanent capital in the trusts. Then the trusts will merely distribute the annual income that the after-tax value of these payments generates. In this way he can most effectively convert deferred compensation payments or distributions from a deferred stock bonus plan into permanent family capital.

THE IRREVOCABLE FAMILY TRUST

This type of trust is created by an individual during his lifetime by an irrevocable transfer of property to the trustee. Essential to this type of trust is that its creator retains none of the rights over the trust income or property that would tax the trust income to him during his life or render the trust taxable for estate tax purposes at his death. If this type of trust is properly designed, it will work "savings" for you in four different ways:

(1) It will effect savings in your income taxes;

(2) It will effect savings in the estate tax and other death charges at your death;

(3) It will effect further savings in the estate tax and other death charges at your beneficiaries' future deaths;

(4) It will eliminate the estate administration expenses that would otherwise be imposed against the trust property at your death.

For these reasons, even though there may be a gift tax, it ordinarily makes sense to use an irrevocable trust. But keep in mind that the more gifts you make, the higher the gift tax rate and the lower your estate tax bracket.

REVERTER TRUST

This type of trust is created by an individual during his lifetime. Its principal distinguishing features are as follows: (1) The life of the trust is expressly limited to a specified term of ten years, a longer period, or for the life of the beneficiary. (2) At the expiration of the specified period, the trust is automatically canceled, and the trust property is then returned to its creator free of the trust.

If you use this type of trust it will effect savings in your income-tax liability during its specified term by removing the income from your taxable income and taxing it to the income beneficiary or the trust itself. However, you must pay a gift tax on the present value of the income gift to the beneficiary to the extent that this value exceeds the gift tax exemptions to which he is entitled.

CHAPTER XIV

SHOULD YOU SET UP TRUSTS AFTER YOUR DEATH

A so-called testamentary trust is one created after an individual's death in accordance with the instructions in his will. Whereas its use will not create any savings at its creator's death or during his lifetime, its use will insulate his property from the otherwise inevitable and successive levies of the estate tax and other death charges as it passes from one beneficiary to another after his death. The elimination of these future charges will create extremely substantial savings for his family.

As we have seen, you can save estate tax on half your estate by leaving it to your spouse outright or in a trust that qualifies for the marital deduction.

The nonmarital deduction property, if left outright to your spouse, will be taxed both in your estate and again in her estate upon her subsequent death unless it is consumed or given away in the period between the two deaths. This means that there is a good possibility that by the time the property reaches your children it will have been depleted by estate taxes in your and your wife's estates.

By placing the property that qualifies for the deduction in a marital deduction trust and the remaining property in a second trust, the maximum marital deduction can be assured and a double estate tax on the nonmarital deduction property avoided.

The second trust, in a typical two-trust arrangement will, will be set up primarily for the protection of the wife during her life without giving her such control over the trust as to make its principal taxable on the wife's subsequent death. Income may be made payable to the wife alone or to the wife jointly with the children. The person creating the trust may restrict himself to setting up one trust out of the residuary estate (or the balance of the residue after the marital deduction is set aside for the surviving spouse), or he may set up a number of trusts, one for each of the children who survive him. Whether the trust is one or more will depend on whether the dollar amount available is sufficient to provide a sound economic funding for more than one trust and whether any tax savings can be provided by an authorization to accumulate excess income.

Here are some objectives and possibilities for this kind of trust:

(1) Income-tax savings may be made available by setting up a separate trust for each child beneficiary so that each trust will be considered a separate taxpayer. This accomplishes a division of the total income among several taxable entities, bringing lower income tax brackets into play.

(2) You may provide that your wife will receive the annual income from the trust property.

(3) However, you may not wish to direct the income to your wife if it will put her into an excessively high income-tax bracket at a time when she will no longer enjoy the benefit of split income. You can, in this case, provide for the accumulation of trust income, state law permitting, or the distribution of trust income to the children and protect your wife by giving your trustee discretion to apply the principal for the support and maintenance of your wife and children if necessary.

(4) The trustee may be directed to "sprinkle" so much of the income of the nonmarital trust among the wife, children,

and grandchildren of the testator as their maintenance and educational requirements dictate.

(5) The ultimate distribution of the principal of the second trust must be specified. You may provide for the distribution of the principal of each of the separate trusts when the child beneficiary attains a specified age (or portions of it at various ages), or you can save further estate tax by deferring distribution of the trust property until the death of the child beneficiary, passing it to grandchildren or surviving sisters and brothers or their descendants if that beneficiary has no children.

(6) You may give each child beneficiary of a nonmarital deduction trust a so-called special power of appointment to grant what remains of his share of the trust at his death among those specified descendants or other relatives: spouses and descendants of the beneficiaries; spouse and descendants of the testator; spouses of any of these descendants. This type of power is tax free.

TESTAMENTARY TRUST IN INCOME PLANNING

The usefulness of trust in minimizing the tax burden on the income from an estate turns on these attributes:

(1) The ability to divide income among beneficiaries and between trust and beneficiaries.

(2) The power to accumulate income and use it for family purposes within the trust.

(3) The ability to give a trustee the discretionary authority to distribute income and capital as the needs and the tax position of the beneficiaries indicate.

The fundamental thing to bear in mind here is that you can set up provisions in a trust for a beneficiary that the beneficiary could not set up for himself without running into tax complications. If a beneficiary created a trust and retained income rights, the property would be includable in his estate. If he directed that trust income be used to carry insurance on his life, the income would be taxed to him. However, if you created the trust for the beneficiary, his right to income would not bring the proceeds into his taxable estate nor would the carrying of insurance on the beneficiary's life make the trust income taxable to the beneficiary.

Here are the kinds of trusts found most useful in income planning for an estate:

RESIDENCE TRUST

The family residence is willed to a trust together with income-producing securities with instructions to the trustee that the wife is to be permitted to use the house rent-free. That income is to be used first to maintain the house, and the balance is to be distributed to the wife. The value of occupancy is not taxed to the wife. Income spent on repairs, insurance, and upkeep of the property will be taxed at lower rates to the trust than to the wife. Income spent by the trust for the wife's enjoyment of the property, including light bills and domestic help, will be taxed to her.

INSURANCE TRUST

Income-producing property is transferred to a trust charged with carrying insurance on for example, a son's life. The income will be taxed to the trust at lower rates than to the son. It will carry more insurance than the same property would support if given to the son outright. Both the income-producing property and the insurance can be kept out of the estates of the son and his wife. Thus, the income placed into such a trust can provide family protection that might require two or three times as many of the son's earned dollars to carry directly.

SPRINKLING TRUST

Here, the trustee is given discretion to accumulate or to distribute income among specified beneficiaries as he thinks best. The income-tax position of beneficiaries will be one of the factors considered in the exercise of this discretion. For example, income can be distributed so that each child gets $1,000 of tax-free money ($600 exemption plus $300 standard deduction plus $100 dividend exclusion) while the balance of the income is accumulated (if allowed by state law) or distributed to a widow who will still have $600 exemptions for her children.

More importantly, the sprinkling trust makes for the use of family income to meet actual family needs as they develop, much as the father of the family does during his life. As a practical matter, an experienced trustee in sprinkling income will be guided by a mother's judgment as to the needs of children, and after the widow's death he will sprinkle unevenly only where there are clear-cut special circumstances, a family consensus, or explicit guidelines in the will creating the trust.

CHAPTER XV

HOW TO EXCHANGE YOUR ESTATE FOR AN INCOME NOW

Frequently, an elderly person will have more capital than he needs. He will be unhappy at the prospect of the size of the lien that his death will attach to his property. Yet he shies away from reducing that lien by making a sizable gift. It may be that he can't bring himself to pay the gift tax now; it may be that he needs the security that the property represents. Either way, the private annuity may provide the answer. It is the one way in which he can reduce his estate and transfer his property without paying gift tax now, capital gains tax now, or estate tax at death.

He transfers property to another person, usually a member of the family, in exchange for that person's promise to pay him an income for life. There is no gift tax if the income is what an insurance company would pay on an annuity costing the current value of the property transferred.

There are legal, financial, and practical problems in tailoring the family annuity transaction to the needs and desires of the family members, but they can be managed. The income produced by the property is shifted to the younger family members—the transferees—and taxed to them. The annual payments they are required to make are not deductible. But the annuitant's cash income position is greatly improved because most of the annual payment is a return of capital and only a small portion is taxable. Any hardship occurring from this imbalance can be alleviated by having the annuitant make annual gifts back to those making the annuity payments.

From the viewpoint of the annuitant, there is another

serious risk involving his lack of security if the person to whom he has transferred his income-producing property sells or otherwise disposes of it. It is true that the annuitant has available to him the usual legal remedies that any party has when a contract is breached. But the tangible benefits to be derived by invoking those remedies will be nil if the other party, having disposed of the property, is without other assets from which to make the annuity payments. Yet at the same time, it may be difficult, as a practical matter, to impose effective restraints on transfers; what is worse, any attempt to impose such restraints in order to provide a security device for the annuitant carries with it the danger that the Internal Revenue Service may regard the security device as a so-called right of reverter, which will render the value of this right includable in the annuitant's estate. These practical difficulties can and have frequently been managed.

The possible tax advantages of a private annuity are:

(1) Income from the property is diverted from a high-bracket taxpayer to one in a lower bracket.

(2) The annuitant will be taxed only on a portion of the payments that he receives.

(3) The annuitant, by reason that gain is not immediately recognized, is able to obtain higher annuity payments than if he had first sold the property and invested the net proceeds (after setting aside an amount for capital gains tax) in a commercial straight life annuity.

(4) The property is removed from the annuitant's estate, thus saving on death taxes, and there is no gift tax on the transfer.

Since the payments will cease upon the annuitant's death, the value of the transferred property will not be included in his estate.

There is no gift as long as the annual income promised

to the annuitant is set at a figure that has the same actuarial value as the value of the property transferred at the time of the transfer. If the annuity promised is below this amount, there is a gift subject to tax, but the annual exclusion ($3,-000) and lifetime exemption ($30,000) may reduce or eliminate any tax liability on the transaction.

Excluded from the annuitant's taxable income each year is an amount found by dividing the value of the transferred property by the annuitant's life expectancy (both factors being fixed as of the date the transaction was entered into). The remaining portion of the annual income is treated as the interest factor in the annuity and is accordingly taxed as ordinary income.

Suppose the property transferred has a fair market value in excess of cost basis to the annuitant. After the annuitant's cost has been returned to him tax free, the same amount as has been recovered tax free in prior years will then be treated as capital gain in each year until such time as the amounts so treated equals the difference between the cost basis of the property and its value at the time of the transfer. Thereafter, apparently, the same amount would then revert to its tax-free status once again. During all this time, of course, the remaining portion of the annual income will be taxed as ordinary income.

Example: how a private annuity works.

Mrs. Smith, age 70, has an estate of $300,000, including a securities portfolio worth some $120,000. Her cost basis for the securities is $80,000. She transfers this portfolio to her son in exchange for his agreeing to pay her $12,000 a year for the rest of her life. What are the tax results to Mrs. Smith?

Estate tax—The estate has been reduced from $300,000 to $180,000, and the potential estate tax from $63,000 to $27,000.

Gift tax—No gift tax. Annual income is as much or slightly more than straight life annuity, which could have been purchased from an insurance company for $120,000.

Income tax—Of the $12,000 annual income, $8,000 is tax-free for 10 years. This figure is arrived at by dividing $120,000 (value of property transferred) by 15 (life expectancy of a female age 70). After the $80,000 cost has been recovered tax-free, then $8,000 a year will be treated as capital gain for the next 5 years until the entire value of the property transferred ($120,000) has been recovered. Then the $8,000 a year will probably become tax-free once again. During all this time, the remaining $4,000 a year, representing the interest portion of the annuity, will always be taxed at ordinary rates.

CHAPTER XVI

PUTTING YOUR FAMILY IN BUSINESS

Perhaps the most economic way to pass wealth to children is to make it for them. A man can't assign his income to his children, but he can lend them money or assets. He can put his skill and experience and energy to work to make assets owned by his children grow in value. There is no income or gift tax on this transfer of skill and energy as there would be if personal earnings were transferred.

More commonly, income is shifted to the members of the family, but that can only be done effectively by transferring ownership of assets that produce income.

The tax savings that arise from the shifting of income within the family come about for the most part because income is transferred from high tax brackets to lower tax brackets. Sometimes, too, an income shift lets us pick up deductions that would otherwise not be available. And, of course, shifting the property that produces the income out of your estate cuts the estate tax. Even if a gift tax is payable, it is lower than the estate tax.

Among the types of property you can give are real estate, stocks, bonds, rental equipment, oil wells, patents, copyrights, a business interest, and so on. Here are some specific illustrations:

(1) If you are receiving income on a contract that doesn't involve your personal services (for instance, an interest in a royalty contract), this may be assigned.

(2) Another type of property that may be assigned is an interest in a nonpersonal service partnership.

(3) If the assignor withdraws completely from any pro-

prietary activities, an entire interest in a business may be assigned even if he continues to advise and do office work.

(4) You may have an interest in a process that is still in the development stage, such as a patent or copyright. If you are an author or inventor, you can give your child or other relative an undivided interest in the copyright or patent. An "undivided interest" means an unseparated part of the whole patent—that is, a piece of all the rights, not a part or whole interest in one or some of the basic rights.

(5) You may be about to retire and sell out of a family corporation. By using a private annuity arrangement in which you transfer your stock in exchange for an equally valued private annuity from your company, you can avoid estate and gift taxes. Also, since the annuity is partly tax exempt, you add to your after-tax income by converting salary to annuity. Incidentally, this is also a good way to shift full ownership of the business to your children.

(6) Another good way of shifting income is to give leasable business property to a low bracket family member. Then, you can enter into a lease, getting business deductions for the rent. *Caution:* the terms must be consistent with those normally found in the field. Otherwise, IRS may question the arrangement. Bear in mind that this type of deal can be made with any type of rental property—not necessarily realty.

(7) You can open a trust account in a bank for your minor child, and the interest paid on such an account will be taxable to the children—if under state law the account legally belongs to the child and the parents are legally prohibited from using any part of the funds to satisfy their support obligations to the child. Or, you can buy securities in the name of your donee (custodian laws let you buy stocks or bonds in the names of your minor children, and in many states other property can be handled in the same way).

SALE OR GIFT AND LEASE-BACK

One way of dividing income within the family is to sell or give business property to family members (directly or in trust) and lease it back. The rent you pay is deductible and the family member or trust that owns the property picks up the rental income.

As an example of the tax saving in the gift or sale and lease-back, take Dr. Skemp's operation. He gave a $40,000 clinic building to a trust for his wife. He was deducting $650 a year for depreciation on the building. After the gift, the trust leased the building to him for $6,000 a year. The doctor's net income ran about $40,000 after deducting the $6,000 rental payment. If he kept the building, he'd have paid an additional $2,600 in income tax at present rates. By shifting the earning power of the building to a trust for children, the tax would be cut down to under $1,000. Thus, there's an annual tax saving of over $1,600 plus the estate tax saving.

The use of an independent trustee can be important in sale- or gift-leasebacks. This helps to show that the donor or seller has parted with all control over the property. What's more important, however, is that both the sales price (where a sale is made) and the rental arrangement stand up as reasonable.

FAMILY PARTNERSHIPS

A family partnership arrangement can fill an important role in the estate plan of an individual business owner. By giving or selling interests in his business to members of his family (particularly children), he can save both income and estate taxes, thereby increasing the family's spendable income and its capital. The problem is to establish the partnership as genuine.

The Code (§ 704(c)) specifically permits us to set up a valid family partnership by gift or purchase even though the partners render no services. In many cases, the family partnership has become clearly preferable to the closely-held corporation from a tax standpoint. In years past, the refusal by the Treasury to recognize many of these partnerships for tax purposes made for great caution in taking advantage of the tax savings possibilities offered by the family partnership. Now, by meeting a clear-cut set of standards, we can use this method of dividing business income with children and other members of the family, bringing much of this income into lower income-tax brackets to increase the family's spendable income and build up its capital too.

FAMILY PARTNERSHIP TAX SAVINGS AND HOW THEY ACCUMULATE

You may be startled at the accumulation of annual income tax savings plus the estate tax saving that can result from creating a family partnership. The following tables will give you an idea of the annual income-tax saving and the cumulative build-up over 20 years, together with the additional tax saving at death. The tax savings are estimated at levels of business income ranging from $25,000 to $300,000 a year. We assume that a father makes a gift of a one-third partnership interest to each of his two children and that the father will report 50 per cent of the partnership income (25 per cent for services and 25 per cent for capital—split up on a joint return with his wife) and the children will report 25 per cent each. The tax savings and the children's income accumulate at 4 per cent compound interest. The estate tax savings are estimated at a 30 per cent rate. You must bear these assumptions in mind in applying the figures to your own situation.

TABLE OF SAVINGS

Net Business Income	Tax as Proprietorship	Family Partnership Tax	Tax Savings Each Year	Tax Savings Over 20 Years
$ 25,000	$ 6,020	$ 4,770	$ 1,250	$ 27,389
50,000	17,060	12,040	5,020	109,993
75,000	30,470	22,030	8,440	184,929
100,000	45,180	34,120	11,060	242,336
150,000	76,980	60,940	16,040	351,452
200,000	110,980	90,360	20,620	451,805
250,000	145,980	121,560	24,420	535,067
300,000	180,980	153,960	27,020	592,035

Tax savings will be even greater if more individuals are taken in as partners.

HOW TO ESTABLISH A FAMILY PARTNERSHIP

You can establish a family partnership in any of these ways—

(1) Accept into partnership any child or other relative who can be expected to perform important work in the business on a regular basis. This is the only sure way of creating a valid family partnership in a professional or personal service firm.

(2) Take into partnership any child or relative who can contribute capital.

(3) Make a gift of a partnership interest to children or other relatives.

(4) Sell a partnership interest to children or other relatives —and the sale can be substantially on credit, to be paid for out of subsequent partnership income.

THE FAMILY INVESTMENT COMPANY

This vehicle has a twofold use—(1) To build the estate by accumulating income at more favorable rates than a high bracket individual can; (2) To shift the value represented by accumulated income and asset appreciation to younger members of the family by giving them common stock while the older generation takes preferred stock for assets put into the corporation.

The family investment corporation can protect income and build common stock values by participating in sale-leaseback, private annuity and partnership arrangements with members of the family. The most dramatic thing it can do is to protect dividend income from the high personal tax rates applicable to the highest individual brackets. Where an individual receives dividend income, the first $100 (up to $200 on a joint return) is nontaxable under the dividend exclusion. Everything over that amount is taxable at rates as high as 70 per cent. Although a corporation gets no dividend exclusion, it does get a deduction for 85 per cent of the dividends it receives. As a result, only 15 per cent of its dividend income is taxable, and that at a maximum rate of 48 per cent. The maximum effective rate is therefore 7.2 per cent (15 per cent x 48 per cent). And where the corporation's taxable income does not exceed the $25,000 surtax exemption, the effective rate can be as low as 3.3 per cent (15 per cent x 22 per cent), or, where you have two or more related companies and multiple surtax exemptions have been elected with the accompanying 6 per cent penalty tax, as low as 4.2 per cent (15 per cent x 28 per cent).

To accomplish these objectives, we have to avoid what is known as personal holding company status for the corporation. If we have a personal holding company, we end up paying a 70 per cent penalty tax or we have to distribute all the corporation's profits to the stockholders (in which case we defeat the whole purpose of using the corporation in the first place since the individuals would then have to pay ordinary tax rates on the distribution).

In any case, the effectiveness of the family investment company has been severely impaired by the Revenue Act of 1964, which tightened up on the available means for avoiding personal holding company problems, and if there is to be any solution for you, skilled professional advice will be needed.

CHAPTER XVII

WAYS TO BENEFIT FAMILY AND CHARITY

By making gifts to charity during life, you can get the benefit of an income-tax deduction as well as getting the property out of your taxable estate. The gift of property, to the extent of the applicable tax rate, builds liquidity as the property is converted into cash in the form of tax savings that remain in the bank instead of being paid to the tax collector.

When property is left to charity under a will, your taxable estate is reduced by the amount of the bequest. And with bequests, you have no problems of dollar limitations. As long as the property goes to a qualified charity, your estate will be entitled to a deduction for estate tax purposes.

Here are some of the estate planning objectives that you can achieve by lifetime charitable gifts:

(1) Build cash or finance life insurance by deducting the value of property given to charity.

(2) Reserve life income for yourself and your wife while converting the remainder interest of the property into tax-saving cash.

(3) Get a lump of tax-saving cash immediately by giving some future investment income to charity.

(4) Getting property and its future appreciation to your children at an actuarially reduced value for gift tax purposes, as well as getting income tax saving cash to pay gift tax, by giving income to charity and remainder interest to children.

(5) Add to gross estate and increase marital deduction by taking insurance out for charity. It may be possible to reserve

incidents of ownership and make the policy payable to charity, increase the amount of property that can be given tax free to your wife and still deduct premium paid to carry insurance for charity.

HOW GIVING PART OF YOUR BUSINESS TO A FOUNDATION PAYS

Where liquidity considerations will force a segment of a business into ownership by a charitable foundation, it is wasteful to have it all occur by bequest at death. A double tax saving is available from a systematic plan of giving a portion of the business to the foundation during each year of life. The subject of the lifetime gifts is effectively removed from the taxable estate. It is also deductible, to the extent of 20 per cent of the giver's income (30 per cent where the foundation is not a private one), on the annual income-tax return. Thus, lifetime gifts, while achieving the same reduction in liability as bequests, also generate additional liquidity since they produce annual savings of cash that would otherwise be payable as income taxes.

Thus, a 50-year old man owns a business worth $1,000,000. His income is $100,000 a year. If he gives $20,000 worth of stock in his company to a foundation, he reduces his annual tax bill from about $55,000 to about $41,000. Thus he increases the cash available to him every year by some $14,000. If he does this for 20 years, he will have built up some $300,000 of liquid assets and will have given 40 per cent of his business to a foundation. He has lost dividends on the stock given to the foundation but the cash tax savings realized each year are more important than the after-tax value of dividends diverted to the foundation.

If he waited for death to direct 40 per cent of his stock to a foundation, his estate would still have only 60 per cent of the business but would be without the $300,000 of liquid capital accumulated from annual income-tax savings.

The amount of liquid capital that can be accumulated for death tax purposes out of such annual income-tax savings will depend on the number of years of life and income left to the owner of a business. A fixed amount of liquid capital at the time needed can be guaranteed by buying life insurance with the income tax cash saved by annual gifts of stock to the foundation.

HOW TO KEEP INCOME AND PROFIT
NOW FROM GIFT TO CHARITY AT DEATH

Sometimes a person may want to help a charity with income-producing property or securities but may feel it necessary to retain the income for his life or for the life of some other person. The charity will accept such a gift and undertake to pay each year to the donor or to some one person designated by the donor, or to one person and, upon the death of that person, to a designated survivor, an annual income determined by applying to the agreed value of the donated property the average net rate of return earned by the charity on its own investment portfolio. Similar results can also be obtained by transferring this property to an irrevocable trust of which the charity is the remainderman, with the trust income being reserved to the donor or someone designated by him.

Under this type of arrangement, the charity does not get any benefit from the property until its obligation to make life income payments terminates. From the charity's viewpoint, it would be just as well if the property were left to it by bequest upon the death of the owner, if income is to be reserved for his life. However, there would be a substantial advantage to the owner in giving the charity the remainder interest during his life, rather than by will or upon his death. He is permitted to deduct on his income-tax return the value of the remainder interest, actuarily computed, that the charity will be receiving.

Example: Mr. Executive is now 60 years old. His wife is 55. His annual income is $120,000. He owns stock now worth $102,500, against his original cost of $25,000. Since most of his income is from compensation and he wishes to retire at 65, he feels that both he and his wife will need the income from the stock or its reinvestment in later years. So Mr. Executive creates a trust with his stock, reserving a life income to himself and, on his decease, to his wife for her surviving lifetime, with the remainder payable to his university.

Here is the economic effect of the plan: Depreciation of the estate of Mr. Executive by reason of the charitable trust— $102,500

Immediate Federal income-tax savings (with the gift spread equally over two years to get the maximum charitable contribution deduction) is—

Tax on $120,000	$57,580	
Tax on $ 96,000	42,780	
	$14,800	

$14,800 times 2 (spread over 2 years) — $29,600

The stock had appreciated by $77,-500. Mr. Executive would not have to pay tax on the capital gain. Had

he sold his stock, the capital gains
tax would have been— $19,375

The charitable deduction for Federal
estate tax purposes at the death of
Mr. Executive would be the then
value of the trust corpus minus the
value of the life estate of Mrs. Executive (assuming her life estate to be
worth $30,000 and that the trust
corpus remains at $102,500). Thus
there would be a deduction of $72,-
500. On a $1,000,000 estate with
marital deduction, the death tax
savings would be— $23,200
                                                        ‾‾‾‾‾‾‾

Total tax savings—assuming no gift
tax payable plus having the advantage of the saved capital gains tax
of $19,375, yielding income for Mr.
and Mrs. Executive for the balance
of their lives. $72,175
                                                        ‾‾‾‾‾‾‾

Net cost of the transaction to the
children and grandchildren of Mr.
and Mrs. Executive— $30,325

The $29,600 of immediate income-tax savings could be the
subject of gifts to children and grandchildren who could
then obtain insurance on the lives of Mr. and Mrs. Executive
(or both) and thereby enjoy tax-free death in excess of
their ostensible loss of inheritance of $30,325.

Diversification of Investment by Charitable Gift
This kind of a transfer permits the donor to convert his

income to that based on a diversified portfolio such as the charity or his trust maintains, without first paying a capital gain tax. Suppose a 60-year old donor in the 50 per cent tax bracket has securities costing him $4,000. They are presently worth $10,000. They are paying him $500 a year, but he would rather diversify his position so that this income is not entirely dependent on a single company or a single property. He could do this by investing in a mutual fund paying him 4 per cent on his then investment. However, in order to shift his investment position to a mutual fund, he would have to pay a capital gain tax of $1,500 so that he would have only $8,500 left to invest. This would give him an annual income of $340 at 4 per cent. By transferring the property to the charity or a trust for a life income, he would get an investment return earned by the charity or trust on its portfolio on the full $10,000. He would also get $3,000 of additional cash (the value of the tax deduction), which could also be invested at 4 per cent. This way, he has an investment return on $13,000, whereas by selling his securities and paying capital gain tax, he has only $8,500 of capital working and producing income for him.

If you want to use this method of diversifying your portfolio to switch into tax exempt securities, you'll meet opposition from the Internal Revenue Service. IRS has taken the position that where the charity receiving the contribution is under an obligation to sell or exchange the property it receives and buys tax exempt securities, it is acting as the donor's agent. In effect, says the ruling, the charity has not received the appreciated property given up by the donor, but has received the proceeds of the sale it made for the donor. Therefore, the donor is taxable on the difference between his basis for the property tranferred and the proceeds of the sale made by the college. IRS concedes that once the property is converted into tax exempt securities, the income remains tax exempt when received by the donor or any one else entitled to the income under the arrangement.

Where property is transferred without any obligation to sell it, a later sale and reinvestment made by the trustee should not cause the person making the gift to have a taxable capital gain.

Gift of Income to Charity and Remainder to Family

Here is how income that will be highly taxed in future years can be converted into immediate cash, with that cash invested in insurance so that the accumulated value of future income is passed over to the family beneficiaries and the property producing the income is transferred to family beneficiaries without estate tax and at an actuarially reduced value for gift tax purposes.

The high-bracket taxpayer creates a trust. He transfers income producing property to the trust, which provides that the income go to the named charity for life or for a specified period of years after which the property is to be distributed to his children. Here is what happens tax-wise:

(1) The donor deducts on his income-tax return the present value of the income dedicated to charity for the term of years specified in the trust.

(2) He has made a taxable gift of the present value of the property at the time the trust terminates as that value is actuarially determined.

(3) When the donor dies, the property goes to his children without an estate tax.

To illustrate, consider a man 55 years old with $100,000 income. He establishes a trust with his $50,000 in securities (which cost him $10,000). He provides that the income will be paid to a designated charity for a period of ten years, at which time the trust will terminate and the securities will be distributed to his son.

This transfer produces $8,680 of additional cash to the person making the gift as shown in the following computation:

Taxable income before contribution	$100,000
Amount of contribution (29.108% of $50,000)	14,554
Tax on income before contribution	45,180
Tax on income after contribution	36,500
Reduction in tax due to contribution	8,680

Thus, $8,680 of tax dollars are generated if the donor has not used up his gift tax exemption. If the taxpayer had used up his gift tax exemption, he would have to pay gift tax on the present value of the property at the end of ten years, which according to Treasury Tables would be $35,446. Gift tax on this would be $2,984, bringing his actual cash saving down to $5,700.

Assuming that the taxpayer will be in a 40 per cent income-tax bracket over the life of the trust and that the $50,000 worth of securities will produce an average annual income of $2,000, the taxpayer will lose $12,000 of income over the ten year life of the trust.

If the cash saving is used to buy a single premium insurance policy he would be able to offset this loss with insurance proceeds.

In the example above, over $10,000 of immediate dollars via tax savings was generated by giving away the income to a charity for ten years.

The following table will show the cash advantage for men in different tax brackets in giving a charity the ten-year income from securities yielding a 4 per cent return and worth $10,000:

Effective Tax Rate of Donor	Aggregate 10-Year Income	Net After Income Tax	Commuted Value of Deduction to Donor	Net Value of Deduction to Donor	Profit If Full Gift Tax Exemption Available
50	$4,000	$2,000	$2,910	$1,455.00	
55		1,800		1,600.50	
60		1,600		1,746.00	$ 146.00
65		1,400		1,891.50	491.50
70		1,200		2,027.50	837.00

Charitable Bequests

When property is left to a charity by will, as long as the charity is a qualified one, the estate gets an estate tax deduction.

It is not necessary that the donor leave the property outright to the charity upon his death. He may want to provide for income to his children or other relatives from the property first. Then, upon their death or attaining a certain age, the property can be transferred to the charity. This is usually done by leaving the property in trust and providing for it to go to the charity upon the termination of the trust (i.e., the charity gets a remainder interest). When a remainder is left to a charity, the deduction allowed for estate tax purposes is less than it would be on an outright gift.

The value of the remainder interest, which enjoys exemption, is determined by multiplying the value of the property by a fraction that varies with the age of life beneficiary. Thus, if the life beneficiary is:

30 years old, 28.129% of the property is exempt
40 years old, 37.092% of the property is exempt
50 years old, 48.020% of the property is exempt
60 years old, 60.321% of the property is exempt
70 years old, 72.630% of the property is exempt

Take a $500,000 estate to be left to a 60-year-old sister. It consists of securities yielding 5 per cent. If it were left outright she would have $370,000 earning 5 per cent after payment of $130,000 in average State and Federal death taxes. That would give her an annual income of $18,500. If she took the $370,000 and purchased an annuity she'd get $21,700 a year, all but $4,100 of it tax exempt. The purchase of an annuity would, of course, consume the entire estate.

If, on the other hand, the $500,000 were bequeathed to her for life and then to a charity, the estate tax would apply to only about $200,000. The estate tax bill would recede to $34,000. She would enjoy annual income of $23,300 and the $500,000 would be preserved for use by a foundation or charity.

CHAPTER XVIII

HOW TO TRANSFER THE MOST AT DEATH

Generally, the biggest item of cost in transferring estate property is the estate tax. The easiest and most convenient way to keep this cost at a minimum is to make a judicious use of the marital deduction, which, as we showed in Chapter XIII, exempts from tax up to 50 per cent of the adjusted gross estate provided it goes to the spouse in a form that qualifies it for the deduction. The marital deduction property will be taxed in the surviving spouse's estate unless consumed or given away during the period between the two deaths. The remainder of the property will be taxed in the first estate but need not be taxed a second time when the surviving spouse dies. She can receive the income from it (and the property itself, if she needs it) without making it a part of her taxable estate simply by having it left in trust for her use but not subject to her control.

Here is how a $26,200 saving in Federal tax works out in a $200,000 estate owned by the husband:

	No Trust	Trust is Used
Gross Estate	$200,000	$200,000
Exemption	60,000	60,000
Net Estate	$140,000	$140,000
Marital deduction	100,000	100,000
Taxable estate when he dies	40,000	40,000
Federal tax	4,800	4,800
Taxable estate when she dies	195,200	100,000*
Federal tax	31,000	4,800

* Plus $95,200 in trust charged with tax payment on husband's death and not taxed on wife's death.

158

METHODS OF TRANSFER BY WILL

An individual may draw his will in many different ways to accomplish his stated objective. Three of the most widely used methods are as follows:

(1) The "Outright" Method—He may leave his estate in its entirety outright to his wife with the expectation that she, in turn, will leave it to the children at her death.

(2) The "Strict Trust" Method—He may direct that all his estate be placed in a trust at his death with the income to go to his wife for life, the property itself to be distributed to his children at her death or some other future date.

(3) The "Marital Deduction-Trust" Method—He may direct that his property be placed in two equal trusts at his death with the income of both to go to his wife for life. The wife must be given the minimal right to direct to whom and how the property in one of the two trusts shall be distributed at her death. (This right or appointive power is necessary to qualify the trust for the "marital estate tax deduction.")

The three methods will produce entirely different death costs. The different costs are illustrated in the examples set out below. The totals given in each case are on the following assumptions:

(1) That the husband's estate will have a value at his death of $250,000.

(2) That his wife has no separate property of her own.

(3) That the estate administration expenses will equal 5 per cent.

(4) That he will predecease his wife.

(5) That she will survive him by ten years.

(6) That his estate will eventually pass to his children.

In computing the totals shown, no effect was given to State estate, inheritance, or succession taxes beyond estimating the

Federal estate tax on a "gross" basis without reduction by the credit for State death taxes.

(1) Under the "Outright" Method—leaving all his property outright to his wife—the approximate death costs will be as follows:

a. At the husband's death $21,688
b. At the wife's death   49,185
c. Total charges over both deaths $70,873

(2) Under the "Strict Trust" Method—putting his estate in an irrevocable trust at his death—the approximate death costs will be as follows:

a. At the husband's death $56,450
b. At the wife's death   None
c. Total charges over both deaths $56,450

(3) Under the "Marital Deduction-Trust" Method—utilizing the marital estate tax deduction in conjunction with trusts—the approximate death costs will be as follows:

a. At the husband's death $21,688
b. At the wife's death   9,188
c. Total charges over both deaths $30,876

To recapitulate, the different tax and expense results of each death are shown below in tabular form:

	Total Death Charges:	Net to Children:
Outright Method	$70,873	$179,127
Strict Trust Method	56,450	193,550
Marital Deduction-Trust Method	30,876	219,124

The "Outright" Method is by far the most costly and expensive of the three methods. It has the futher possible disadvantage of directly thrusting all the intricate problems of property and securities management on the wife at the husband's death. Both factors, or one of the two, usually lead to the abandonment of the "Outright" Method of property distribution by an individual who is apprised of its drawbacks. This leaves for consideration the "Strict Trust" and "Marital Deduction-Trust" methods.

In approaching these other methods, the advantages and possible disadvantages of each should be carefully weighed. Under the "Strict Trust" method, the husband will gain the absolute assurance that his estate will pass to his children at some future designated date. He will thereby eliminate any possibility that any part of his property will be diverted to anyone but his children. Moreover, through the terms of the trust, he will be able to impress his own personal wishes and instructions indelibly on the trust property and income and thereby gain the further assurance that his children will ultimately receive the whole of his estate. Under the "Marital Deduction-Trust" approach he would have to give his wife the minimum right to direct to whom and how roughly one-half of his estate shall be distributed at her death. This may well prove to be an inconsequential hazard in many husband-wife situations but a factor to be reckoned with in others.

Care must be exercised whenever leaving a life estate to a spouse that a nondeductible terminable interest has not been created. This is an interest that will fail or terminate on the lapse of time or on the occurrence or nonoccurence of some contingency. However, not all terminable interests are disqualified for the marital deduction.

CHAPTER XIX

WHAT YOUR WILL SHOULD DO

Rely on a good lawyer to convert your desires for your beneficiaries and your property into an effective will. There is an infinite variety of detail that should be considered and discussed before the preparation of a will. Some lawyers have a preliminary questionnaire that they ask their clients to fill out and answer before the first office conference. This will enable you to put together basic data about yourself, your family, and your assets and liabilities, and at the same time it will provide you with a checklist of documents to be assembled and brought to your lawyer's office. See the specimen form of questionnaire in the Appendix.

Much of the detail required in planning your will comes out of your own experience, your appraisal of your property and your heirs, and your aspirations for them. Beyond the details called for in the preliminary questionnaire, there are some technical matters on which you should develop your own ideas so that you can discuss them properly with your lawyer.

The following series of questions provides a useful check to stimulate your thinking prior to the preliminary conversation with your lawyer:

Any Special Instruction for *Funeral Arrangements, Upkeep of Cemetery Plot, and so on?* Instructions can be spelled out in your will. Burial instructions in a will are useless where the provisions of the will remain secret until some date after death and after burial has already taken place. The matter can be left to the discretion of your family, or you may leave a special letter addressed to your executor or to your family to acquaint them with your wishes.

Who Should Get Your Personal Belongings?—If you do not provide for the disposition of clothing, jewelry, furniture, and so on, such articles, unless state law provides otherwise, will go into what is known as the residue of your estate (what is left after debts, taxes, costs, specific legacies, etc. have been paid) and possibly impose on your executor the obligation to sell them. Tangible personal property should always be disposed of by separate will provisions. This is because under the Internal Revenue Code all amounts distributed to a beneficiary for the taxable year must be included in the gross income of the beneficiary to the extent of the distributable net income of the estate. However, any amount that under the terms of the will is distributed as a gift of specific property all at once or in not more than three installments is excluded. If the tangible personal property is separately disposed of in the will and is distributed to the legatee all at once, its distribution will have no income-tax consequences. However, if disposed of as part of the residue, its distribution might be taxable as income to the legatee. It may be wise to specify the individuals who are to receive the most valuable of your personal possessions and leave the balance to someone in whom you have confidence, with instructions to divide them at his discretion among those close to you.

Do You Want to Make Any Cash Bequests?—When you leave a specific amount of money to an individual or to a charity, your executor is required to pay that amount in full before he makes any distribution to the beneficiaries who are to share the balance of your estate. If your estate should be smaller than you expect, such a cash bequest could result in your unintentionally having made inadequate provision for other beneficiaries. You can guard against this by providing that cash bequests shall be paid only if the total estate exceeds a specified minimum. Or bequests to individuals and charities can be made in fractions or percentages of the estate, rather than in fixed dollar amounts.

What Do You Want to Do With Your Real Estate?—Do you want to leave your solely owned real estate outright, place it in trust (possibly a residence trust in which your wife has the rights to the house), have it sold and the proceeds distributed, give one beneficiary—for example, your wife—the right to use it for life with ownership going to your children on her death? Under the law of some states, your spouse may have what are known as dower or curtesy rights in your real estate. These rights may vary from state to state.

Do You Want to Leave an Income for Anybody?—You may want to assure a regular income for your parents, dependent relatives, or others. You may do this through a trust established by will or by directing your executors to buy annuities for named beneficiaries. In the event that you establish the trust, you can specify the individual to whom the trust property will go after it has produced the required income for a specified period of time.

Whom Do You Want to Have the Remainder of Your Estate?—Decide who is to share in the bulk of your estate. Then divide the balance, after specific bequests, in fractions or percentages. By being overly exact in allocating particular assets to certain beneficiaries, or in specifying interests in dollar amounts, you can frustrate your own objectives in the event of important changes in the size or value of your estate. If you divide the bulk of the estate by fractions of a share, you won't be in a position of having to revise your will repeatedly because of changes in asset values. Be sure your will names alternate or contingent beneficiaries who are to receive the share of any beneficiary who fails to survive you.

What Can You Do to Protect the Interests of Minor Bene-

ficiaries?—It is usually necessary to have a guardian appointed by the court to manage the child's property until he or she attains the age of 21. The guardian must furnish bond, make periodic accountings, and secure court approval on many of the actions he will have to take. Guardianship, except for small sums of money, can be both burdensome and expensive. Your will can simplify this matter by directing the property be turned over to a trust to be held for the benefit of minors until majority. The trustee can be authorized to use the trust property to provide maintenance, support, and education for the minor.

What Can You Do to Protect the Interest of Adult Beneficiaries?—Adult beneficiaries can dissipate outright gifts quickly. You should decide whether you want to leave your property outright, turn it over to beneficiaries in installments, or have it held and managed for their benefit by an experienced trustee.

How Do You Want Trust Property Handled?—Subject to local law, you can determine whether the income of trust property is to be distributed or accumulated in order to build up future value. You can determine how much of the income is to be distributed and how much of it is to go to each beneficiary. You can authorize the trustee to distribute some of the trust principal to your beneficiaries if income is insufficient to maintain living standards or meet emergencies. Again subject to local law, you can decide when the trust is to terminate—for example, whether it should be distributed to your children or held for your grandchildren. You should decide at what age your beneficiaries should be capable of handling the property themselves. You may wish to have them receive trust principal gradually in installments.

Whom Do You Want as Executor and Trustee?—An executor and possibly a trustee must be designated to handle the settlement and management of your estate. This responsibility must be accepted. The details of settling an estate must be handled. Your property must be managed until it is turned over to your beneficiaries. These are tasks that call for a high degree of skill and experience. The choice of an executor and trustee may determine whether your plans for your family and your property will succeed or fail.

Other Points to Consider—Even if you have a will, changes in the law and new developments in your own affairs may have made your will obsolete. Here are points you should discuss with your lawyer unless you have reviewed them very recently—

(1) Does your will take full advantage of the marital deduction, which can exempt as much as half of your estate from tax?

(2) Are your insurance arrangements integrated with your will? (See the checklist for integration in Chapter XI).

(3) Are inheritance taxes to be paid by each beneficiary or by the estate?

(4) Should your executor have authority to carry on your business, or should he be directed to dispose of it?

(5) Have safeguards been established to minimize the possibility that your property will be taxed twice—once when you die and again when your wife dies?

(6) Has provision been made for the possibility that you and your wife may die under such circumstances that it is impossible to determine which one died first?

(7) Does your executor have the right to borrow money, to pledge estate assets, and to renew existing obligations?

(8) Should your executor have the power to retain real estate or sell, mortgage, or lease it?

(9) Should your executor have the right to retain assets owned by you at the time of your death, whether or not they

are so-called legal investments for trust and estate funds?

(10) Does your trustee have broad discretion in the investment and reinvestment of trust funds? Do you want to give him any specific instructions?

(11) Have income provisions for trust beneficiaries been protected against inflation?

(12) Does the trustee have the right to make special provision for beneficiaries in the event of emergencies?

(13) Will there be enough liquid funds to meet estate tax obligations and other cash requirements that will confront your executor and trustee?

(14) Has the future distribution of your property been studied with a view to minimizing the tax drain on the income it will produce?

BE SURE TO PROVIDE FOR CONTINUED FAMILY INCOME

When the breadwinner dies, it takes time to get the executor appointed and to inventory the estate. Then the executor may want to defer the creation of any trust and any significant distributions from the estate until tax liabilities have been ascertained and met. Even after trusts are set up, it takes time for them to accumulate income. Many wills make a serious oversight in failing to make sure that the widow will have sufficient income for her own support and that of the children during this period. Here are some of the steps that should be considered to relieve this possibly embarrassing situation:

(1) If the widow could keep in her own name sufficient cash and liquid assets that together with insurance proceeds coming to her directly would cover the cost of living for herself and the family for a two-year period, there would be no

problem at all. Her joint-account securities and bank deposits will also be available for this purpose. In most states, the bank account and the transfer of securities will be blocked at the death of one of the joint tenants, but withdrawals and transfers can then be made simply on the presentation of a state death tax waiver and death certificate.

(2) The creation of an inter vivos or living trust that will be in operation immediately upon the husband's death and from which current income and capital can be distributed to tide the family over the period of estate administartion.

(3) Most states attempt to solve this difficulty by a statutory provision that gives the widow a forced legacy, payable periodically for a certain period after death, out of the husband's property. These are the widow's awards, or allowances. Sometimes this is inadequate, and this can be supplemented by providing in the will that the wife is to get a continuing legacy of so many dollars a month commencing with the date of death. The executor will be directed to pay this sum each month until a distribution of a specified size is made from the estate or until a trust created by the will is set in motion to make regular income payments. For the sake of clarity, the will should direct that this continued legacy is not to be charged against income from the trust.

(4) Have the will provide that the income of any trust to be established under the will is to accrue from the date of death. The laws of many states provide that income earned by the estate during the period of administration will accrue to residuary legatees and a residuary trust proportionately unless another disposition is made by the will. Where this is the rule, either by state law or by explicit direction of the will, the will might further provide that until the trusts are set up the executor is to have the discretion to make to the wife (as advance payments of income from the general

estate) such payments as the executor computes to be equal to the income that is currently accruing to the trust that will be set up later for the widow's benefit. The will might further provide that additional principal advances may be made to the widow, and that any such payments made from principal during the period of administration should be added back to trust principal from trust income after the trusts are functioning. This recoupment should be spread out for a sufficient period of time so that the widow will not have her cash difficulties simply postponed, instead of solved. In making advances to the widow before the period for the presentation of claims has expired, the executor must protect himself against the claims of creditors to which he would be responsible to the extent of distributions made to other persons. This may be done by getting some kind of a refunding bond from the widow so that the distributions made to her and needed for creditors can be recovered. The same thing is true of any advance payments made to the widow from principal that are to be recouped later from income that becomes distributable to the widow.

WHERE DO YOU LIVE?

An estate owner may spend his winters in Florida, summers in Maine, and commute between New York and Washington, D.C. during the rest of the year, maintaining residences of a more or less permanent nature in all four places. Which of these jurisdictions shall be his domiciliary state for purposes of will probate, estate administration, and the like? It could be that potential administration expenses in his estate would be considerably less in one jurisdiction than in any of the others. All other things being equal, he would probably prefer that this state be treated as his domicile, inasmuch as the legality and administration of his will and estate are determined by the laws and practice of the domiciliary state. And what about inheritance taxes? To which state should they be paid? Or can part be paid to one state and part to another?

All discussions of domicile center on one question: *Where is your principal home?* And in many cases, this question is easier asked than answered. The solution lies in a two-pronged affirmative approach: (a) Assert which state you wish to be your domicile; (b) Act accordingly. Observe these rules.

(1) Integrate your activities to coincide with your assertion as to your state of domicile. If necessary, adjust your pattern of living if it will give added weight to an otherwise questionable choice of domicile.

(2) Label your choice of domicile as *your home, your legal residence, your address,* reserving to the others such titles as *summer home, winter home, vacation home, business home,* etc. Recite your domicile in your will.

(3) File *resident tax returns* in the state you select for your domicile, nonresident returns in the others.

(4) Keep the bulk of your valuable assets within your claimed domiciliary state. Not only is this further evidence of your intentions, it is also a much easier and less expensive matter for your personal representative to collect and distribute such property than if it had been scattered.

(5) Consider whether it is advisable to hold on to real estate in any state other than your claimed domicile. Not only may this bring up the question of what is your domicile, it may also involve costly ancillary proceedings.

(6) Use the address of your claimed domicile for purposes of bank accounts, automobile and driver's licenses, securities registration and dividend payment notices, life insurance, etc.

(7) Register and vote where you wish to be domiciled.

(8) File for homestead or veterans' real estate tax exemptions in the state in which you assert your domicile.

CHAPTER XX

HOW TO PICK
YOUR PERSONAL REPRESENTATIVE

Your executor or trustee has to assume responsibility and liability. He must act for you in the interest of your family. Look for these qualities:

(1) *Integrity.* This might be termed the one indispensable ingredient of a good fiduciary. If you can't rely implicitly on his loyalty and honesty in carrying out your wishes, then the purpose of your careful estate planning may be defeated.

(2) *Responsibility.* This is companion to the quality of integrity. By years of labor and planning, the estate owner presumably has built up what he considers adequate provision for the support and comfort of his family. But his labors can come to nought if his estate is dissipated through irresponsible management after his death.

(3) *Experience.* The kind of experience you will look for in a fiduciary will depend on the assets that make up the estate. You think of a businessman if there is a business to be continued, liquidated, or sold. You think of a man who has managed or owned real estate where there are large real estate holdings, an investment counselor in an estate of stock and bond holdings. But a trust company either now has or has the capability of acquiring any of these skills as well as others that may be needed.

(4) *Sympathy.* An estate is "property" only in a limited sense. More broadly, it is a means for taking care of the needs and wants of beneficiaries. Unless a fiduciary can provide sympathy and understanding for the beneficiaries he will not be able to fully meet these needs and wants.

(5) *Availability.* To determine the availability of a candidate for a fiduciary role, we must answer two questions: (1)

Will he be around enough? (2) Will he be around at all? A fiduciary whose business or profession keeps him traveling a lot may not always be on hand to attend to important matters as they arise or to meet developing emergencies. And a man who is older than the estate owner may not be alive to serve at all. Or if he is alive, he may be living in retirement, too far out of touch with everyday affairs to be suitable for the estate's needs.

(6) *Willingness.* Even if the man we want has all of the above qualities, they will not help if he is unwilling to accept appointment. Therefore, the first step is to find out whether the man you want is willing to serve.

Individual or Corporate Fiduciary

The most compelling reason for naming an individual as fiduciary is the feeling that a particular individual has special knowledge, special experience, special familiarity and special understanding of the problems and needs of your business and family. You may think that a corporate fiduciary will be timid and overconservative with respect to your business affairs. You may find it difficult to visualize a financial organization serving in the role of parent toward your children.

On the other hand, relatively few individuals are equipped with the experience to carry out the many complicated and technical chores that are required of a fiduciary, particularly if the estate or a portion of it is to be continued in a trust. They do not get the accumulated experience that a professional fiduciary develops. Individuals die. Health and competing interests may not permit adequate attention and continued availability for the fiduciary task. A family member or friend may easily have or develop conflicting interests. Most individuals do not have enough financial responsibility to protect the beneficiaries against the financial loss that may result from mishandling; as a gesture of confidence to the individuals named in a fiduciary capacity, many will direct that the posting of a surety bond be waived. Few individuals have the sheer administrative facilities to handle an estate systematically and properly.

The arguments for a corporate executor-trustee may be summed up as follows:

(1) It specializes in the handling of estates. The individual does not. It can give full time and attention to the estate; the individual will be distracted by his own business and personal affairs.

(2) It is experienced and responsible. Its work represents the combined knowledge and judgment of many seasoned men.

(3) Its information and experience enable it to manage property so as to conserve the full value thereof for the benefit of the heirs.

(4) It is fair, impartial, and obedient to the directions of the will and trust instrument. The individual often finds it hard to handle the delicate situations that frequently arise in which personal wants and discretionary powers are involved.

(5) It takes over the affairs of an estate or trust as a matter of business. A friend or relative usually is not conversant with such details and finds them a burden.

(6) The corporate fiduciary never dies. The individual does, often with his work unfinished.

Does the personal interest in the welfare of the heirs, personal knowledge of your business, and personal concentration that a particular individual can bring to the administration of an estate and trust outweigh the greater experience, superior facilities, and assured impartiality of the corporation? This is something for you to decide, bearing in mind that death may deprive him of the qualities sought in the selection of the individual while you can be reasonably sure a corporation will endure. They usually declare that they are to exist in perpetuity.

When a trust is involved, the setting up of a trust under the will furnishes a compelling argument for the naming of a corporate fiduciary as both executor and trustee. Administration will be more sound and orderly if the party who administers the property as an estate continues administering it after it has gone into the trusts. The trustee's job is largely the day-to-day exercise of business judgment in managing the assets of the trust and making changes in the investments needed to maintain principal values and produce adequate income.

Because of its greater experience, wider access to information, and superior facilities, a corporate fiduciary is better suited than an individual in the carrying out of the trustee duties. Even if the individual who might be selected has the necessary business judgment and knowledge to do the job properly today, it isn't likely that you could count on these qualities being available throughout the life of the trusts.

Individual and Corporate Fiduciaries Serving Jointly

The problem of whether to choose an individual or corporate fiduciary may be solved by choosing both. A combination of an experienced corporate fiduciary and a relative or friend, acting together, may be preferable to either one acting alone. Even if the friend or relative is qualified to do the job alone, he may be unwilling to take on sole responsibility. He may be willing, however, to serve jointly with a corporate fiduciary better equipped than he to discharge the administrative burdens and with which he can share the responsibilities.

The combination can work very well in some cases, with the corporate fiduciary furnishing the experience and necessary facilities and the individual contributing insight into the workings of the estate owner's mind. A corporate fiduciary will seldom be as well equipped as an intimate family friend or relative for "reading between the lines" of the will or trust to discover what motivated the estate owner in granting a particular discretion and how he intended it to be exercised. There may be personal or business reasons why he chose to cover the matter in a discretionary provision, rather than by express direction.

In this case, appointment of the individual as co-executor and/or trustee will give the estate owner assurance that his true wishes will be fulfilled.

Risks in Naming Co-Fiduciaries

The naming of a co-fiduciary, however, may have certain disadvantages. For one thing, it means extra expense, since there will be two fees instead of one. There is also the danger that disagreement between the fiduciaries may mean delay in making necessary decisions; in general, administration may be made more cumbersome.

All things considered, it will probably be better not to appoint two fiduciaries if the objective sought can be achieved some other way. In deciding this point, the estate owner might ask himself these questions.

(1) For the settlment of my estate and the subsequent management of my property, do I need more than one fiduciary?

(2) If so, what do I expect the two fiduciaries to accomplish that one acting alone could not accomplish as well?

(3) If I name more than one fiduciary, do I want each of them to act jointly on everything connected with my estate, or do I want one of them to do certain things and the other or others to do other things?

(4) If I have in mind special duties for each of them, shall I state the duties and powers of each of them separately, so that each of them may know his part?

(5) What provision shall I make for the compensation of each, so that each will be paid adequately and fairly for the services he renders?

(6) Is there any other arrangement than having joint fiduciaries—such as advisers to a sole fiduciary or separate fiduciaries—that will accomplish what I have in mind better than joint fiduciaries would accomplish it?

CHAPTER XXI

SINS AND PITFALLS

The implementation of any estate plan calls for professional skill and know-how. It is no job for do-it-yourself amateurs. The American Bar Association through the Council of its Section of Real Property, Probate and Trust Law has called attention to the peril that resides in the do-it-yourself approach. It has said that "there is no way of resolving the problems of the great multitude of persons through the use of a single, simple, stereotyped form any more than one could cure all illnesses with a single pill."

In this chapter we will spell out the seven cardinal sins of estate planning and then detail twenty-nine specific pitfalls that can be encountered in the do-it-yourself approach to estate planning.

THE SEVEN CARDINAL SINS

These are the big mistakes than can create financial disaster, freeze an estate so that it cannot meet the needs of its beneficiaries, nullify and even reverse your intention, or tie up your estate in the courts for years. The only practical protection against these perils is an experienced lawyer who will assume responsibility for implementing your estate plan.

1. Letting the legislature or the courts write or rewrite your will: You certainly let the legislature write your will when you die without a will. You may let the legislature rewrite your will when your will fails to spell out your intentions with respect to children born after your death; when your will fails to specify what is to happen if a legacy fails or when a beneficiary dies; or when your will, relying on a provision of state law that the legislature can change, fails to spell out matters of procedure and authority, and so on.

It can happen whenever there is a violation of the rule against perpetuities.

The courts may write or rewrite your will when it is drafted with such imprecision that it lends itself to more than one interpretation. It can then become necessary to call on the probate court to determine the proper meaning, sometimes at great cost in time, money, loss of opportunity to liquidate or to take advantage of options and other valuable elections, and so on. Examples of this kind of imprecision are manifold. For example,

. . failure to specify the time when a determination is to be made

. . failure to specify which wife, children by which marriage, of the blood or by adoption, legitimate or illegitimate

. . talking about heirs without specifying by what law and as of what time

. . failure to provide for the disposition of the interest of those who predecease the testator

2. *Letting the family bear the burden of adversity:* Many men, feeling flush, bequeath handsome sums to their pet charities, employees, friends, and relatives and then direct that the balance (the residue) be set up or distributed to take care of their family. If adversity strikes, before or after death, the bequests expressed in dollar amounts stand, and the family assumes all the loss. For example, a man thinks he is worth a million dollars and bequeaths $100,000 to alma mater. At death, it turns out that he's worth $200,000. Alma mater gets more than half of his estate, and his family gets $100,000 less taxes, less than 15 percent of what he intended. This should never be permitted to happen and will not if bequests are properly conditioned on the size of the estate or limited to a percentage of the estate.

3. *Bankrupting the estate:* This can easily happen if

large amounts, on which taxes must be paid, are permitted to go to beneficiaries outside of the estate while, under state law or the provisions of the will, the residue passing under the will bears the burden of taxes. Tying up a lot of insurance in installment payments so that the funds are not available to pay taxes is another way to bankrupt the estate.

4. *Letting the marital deduction throw you:* There are two ways to do this:

a. fumbling the ball by creating a terminable interest or leaving your wife unproductive property or not giving her sufficient control over the property so that the opportunity to pass half the estate tax free is lost.

b. reaching for the tax saving at the risk of half your property going to your wife's second husband.

You have to know your wife and make your decision. The tragedy is not making the wrong decision but not taking a good look at the two alternatives. You should at least know what it will cost to put your property out of the reach of your wife's next husband.

5. *Putting the money on ice:* You can freeze your estate so that it can't be used for your own needs or those of your family by putting it into an irrevocable trust during your life or into a trust created by your will without authorizing access to the principal. This can be avoided by giving the trustee or a designated advisor the right to dip into capital to meet specified needs or to even terminate the trust. Further flexibility can be provided, without adverse tax consequence, by giving the beneficiaries the right, on their own initiative, to draw down limited amounts of principal (5 per cent or $5,000 or enough to maintain living standards).

6. *Failing to protect your heirs from themselves:* This is the reverse of sin No. 5. You can commit it by letting children have substantial amounts of free capital before they have the maturity to handle it. There are a lot of people eating well today only because father arranged things so that some portion of his capital never became freely and fully available to his children and grandchildren for consumption or investment but remained in trust to produce annual income for them.

7. Picking a representative who is either inadequate or inadequately authorized: The easiest way to do this is to name as executor a friend who will not have the time, the experience, or the inclination to handle your affairs. Sometimes this is done as a favor or to recognize loyalty and friendship. All too often, it is the worst thing you can do to a friend harassed by his own problems. It can be cruel to leave a wife with the burden of estate administration and investment.

Even if you pick the right executor, his hands can be tied if your will fails to give him authority to continue a business, retain investments, borrow money, and take other steps called for. You can paralyze his judgment and initiative by not providing not only authority but also exoneration for mistakes of judgment.

29 PITFALLS IN THE DO-IT-YOURSELF APPROACH

The following examples illustrate a few pitfalls that lie in the path of estate owners who choose to do their own planning or use an advisor who is unqualified in this vast and intricate field. All of them stem from actual cases and rulings.

1. The Unexpected Gift: Husband heard that if he transferred the ownership of his insurance to his wife it would escape tax in his estate. What he didn't know was that proceeds payable to beneficiaries other than the new owner would be treated as a taxable gift!

2. Joint Property Taxed Twice: In order to avoid probate, husband transferred property into his and his wife's names as joint owners. No one told him that the full value of the jointly held property would be included in the estate of the first joint owner to die to the extent that the surviving joint ower could not prove contribution toward the purchase price. Although wife had property of her own, she paid nothing toward the jointly held property. Nevertheless, the full value of this property was included in her estate since husband's records were inadequate.

3. *Lost Opportunity Under* § *303:* Husband was the owner of a successful business. In order to avoid probate, on as much of his company stock as possible, he made periodic gifts of the stock to his wife. These gifts dropped his interest in the company stock below 35 per cent of his gross estate and 50 per cent of his taxable estate. *Result:* The benefits of IRC §303 were not available. The estate lost the opportunity to siphon off corporate earnings at capital gain rates in redemption of his stock.

4. *Lost Opportunity Under* § *6166:* Same facts as the prior pitfall. *Result:* Since husband's interest in the corporation fell below the 35 per cent and 50 per cent tests, it failed to qualify for the benefits of IRC §6166. This section permits the estate to spread the payment of estate taxes over a ten-year period.

5. *The Gift Boomerang:* A good way of reducing husband's probatable and taxable estate is to make gifts to the persons who would ultimately receive the property anyway. If husband is a do-it-yourself estate planner, chances are the property selected for the gift will be his house. However, if he continues to live in the house, IRS would insist that it be included in his estate for tax purposes under § 2036 (transfers with retained life interest). Husband's estate may win the point after a long expensive court battle; but legal advice would avoid this course in favor of less expensive alternatives.

6. *Employee Benefits Subjected to Tax:* Husband has

an interest in a qualified pension plan. He figures that he might as well name his estate beneficiary so all his assets will be administered together. Had he sought proper advice, he would have been made aware of the fact that these benefits will be subject to tax unnecessarily under IRC §2039(c).

7. *Lost Charitable Deduction:* Assume the same facts as the preceding pitfall, except here the beneficiary is husband's favorite charity. Since the plan is qualified, none of the benefits will be included in his estate, and therefore, under § 2055, the charitable deduction will be lost. He could have been advised to make his charitable gift from taxable property that would be offset by the deduction. The employee benefits would then pass to the beneficiary, who would have otherwise received the taxable property less taxes.

8. *Nontaxables Unnecessarily Taxed to Wife:* Same facts as the preceding two pitfalls, except assume that the beneficiary is husband's wife. Although the benefits aren't taxable in husband's estate, they will be taxable in wife's estate upon her subsequent death, thus increasing her taxes and probate expenses. This problem can be avoided by making the benefits payable to a trust in which the wife has a special power of appointment.

9. *The Wrong Power of Appointment:* Suppose husband has heard of the trust suggested in the preceding pitfall and decides to use a "do-it-yourself" trust form to set it up. If wife has what amounts to a general power of appointment— that is, the right to appoint to herself, her estate, her creditors, or the creditors of her estate—it will all have been for nothing. Properly advised, husband will permit her to appoint to anybody but these four. This will give her flexibility without subjecting the property to tax.

10. *Exercise of a Pre 10-21-42 Power:* While we are on the subject of powers, suppose husband's or wife's parents had

transferred property in trust subject to a general power created before October 21, 1942. Husband may be expected to exercise his power in favor of his beneficiaries. We know, however, that such exercise will cause the property to be included in his estate while ignoring it in favor of the takers in default (usually the same beneficiaries anyway) will exempt this property from taxation.

11. Another Gift Boomerang: Parent makes gifts to his children to reduce both income and estate taxes. He makes the mistake of being custodian of the gift property. When parent dies, IRS will throw this property right back in his taxable estate under IRC § 2036 or 2038.

12. The Dangers of An Amateur Executor: Husband wants to save the executor's fees by appointing his wife executrix. Since she has had little or no experience in marshaling, appraising, administering, and completing the numerous duties of an executor, an advisor could point out the myriad pitfalls that lie in her path.

13. The Dangers of an Amateur Trustee: Husband decides to be the trustee of trusts created for his children. He has never heard about the prohibitions against self-dealing, exchanging assets, commingling funds, and the many other fiduciary responsibilities of a trustee. In many cases his mistakes won't come to light. In others, the children grow up, marry, argue with Dad and drag him into court to get what is rightfully theirs. Perhaps Dad should have talked to a lawyer or trust officer before he "did-it-himself."

14. Gifts of the Wrong Property: Sure, Dad can avoid probate by making gifts of his property before he dies. But what property should he give? We have already seen the pitfalls of giving away too much of his family business. But even more costly tax-wise would be a gift of low basis property when Dad is old and the property may get a new basis equal to the estate tax value.

Still worse is the gift of property that has a basis higher than the property's fair market value. In this case the donee has to use the fair market value as the basis while the difference between fair market value and Dad's cost is lost forever as an income offset. Does Dad plan to make any gifts to charity? Does he have an § 306 stock? Is he forced to sell some low basis property to meet current obligations? There is a right way and a wrong way to handle each situation. There is no substitute for sound advice in this area.

15. *Loss of Stock Appreciation:* Husband quits his job holding a bundle of qualified stock options. The plan provides that the option must be exercised within 90 days after the termination of employment but at least within 5 years from date of grant. Perhaps he read his stock option contract or maybe the employer told him about the need for prompt exercise. More likely than not, during the uncertain period after his termination, the exercise of these options, which will require a substantial cash outlay, is the furthest thing from his mind. But, without some advice on the subject, the unrealized stock option appreciation is apt to disappear forever on the 91st day. Whenever there is a major change in the family situation, be it property values, employment, marital status, or whatever, a complete estate planning review is vital.

16. *Domicile Problems:* Husband makes a few dollars and buys a winter home in Florida. He spends about six months of the year in Ohio and six months in Florida. After ten years of shuttling back and forth, about half his estate is in each place. Apart from running the risk of double taxation, the administration expenses will be higher owing to the duplication of administration procedures. Often the cost of expert advice on this subject before husband dies will be saved many times over after his death.

17. *Common Disaster Problems:* Dad read a book on

how to write your own will. The form suggested and used by him provided that in the event he and his wife died as the result of a common disaster, his secondary beneficiaries would take. This it was said would avoid two administrations. The book ignored the loss of the marital deduction but that didn't matter because the estate was below the exemptions. He and his wife were involved in a serious auto accident. He died the next day. His wife was still in the hospital with her injuries two years later. In the meantime the estate was still open since if she were to die it might still be considered to have been as a result of a common disaster in which case Dad's secondary beneficiaries would take under his will.

18. *The Backfiring Payment of Debts Clause:* Same facts as the preceding pitfall, except that here the form used by Dad contained a standard clause found in most boiler-plate forms directing the executor to "Pay all my just debts and funeral expenses as soon after my demise as possible." Fifteen years ago Dad had his debts discharged in bank-ruptcy; certain other debts have become uncollectible as the result of the statute of limitations. Unfortunately, the courts in Dad's state of domicile have held that all debts are revived by such a direction in the debtor's will.

19. *Other Debts Clause Problems:* Same facts as the preceding pitfalls, except here assume that he has a low-interest mortgage on his house. The inclusion of this clause in the will forces the executor to pay off the mortgage when actually the beneficiaries may prefer to keep the mortgage in force and invest the money at a higher rate of interest. Again, suppose he has a loan on his insurance policy that he expects to be paid out of the policy itself (not too uncommon these days with minimum deposit and bank loan insurance). A payment of debts clause will force the executor to pay the insurance loan out of the property in the estate to the det-riment of his residuary beneficiaries.

20. *Income in Respect of a Decedent:* Client never heard of income in respect to a decedent. How could he possibly know that the estate tax credit available under 691(c) will be lost if this property is left to his wife and qualifies for the marital deduction.

21. *Pitfalls of Business Continuation; Associate Dies First:* When Dad's co-50%-stockholder died, he never dreamed that his associate's surviving wife would be such a problem. Differences of opinion have brought the business to a standstill. She wants dividends; he wants to expand. A funded buy-sell or stock redemption agreement would have avoided this problem.

22. *Pitfalls of Business Continuation; Husband Dies First:* Husband's company paid him a good salary but never paid a dividend. He dies and wife receives his 50 per cent interest. Unfortunately, she no longer draws husband's salary, and the stock is a frozen asset with no dividends.

23. *Pitfalls of Business Continuation; the Problem of Paying Taxes:* Same facts as the preceding pitfall, except that here part of husband's interest had to be sold to pay his taxes. Now his survivors become minority stockholders. This effects not only their control but reduces the value of their stock. Expert advice may have avoided these problems.

24. *Income Tax on Insurance:* When husband, a great believer in life insurance, hears that his brother-in-law is about to let his policy lapse, he offers to pay brother-in-law an amount equal to the cash value in return for ownership of the policy. Husband takes over the policy and leaves his sister as beneficiary. Two weeks later brother-in-law dies. *Result:* Gift for Federal tax purposes from husband to sister for the entire face value of the policy. But even more painful, the difference between the cash value paid to brother-in-law and the death value is subject to ordinary income tax in husband's top bracket (IRC § 101(a)).

25. *Pitfall of Procrastination:* Husband is pretty much the same as all of us. Until we have an expert to point out the many problems that will confront our loved ones and the opportunities for accomplishing our objectives, we tend to put off what must be done. If there is one pitfall that has cost the beneficiaries of decedents more in terms of grief and cold hard cash, it is procrastination. Husband heard that he could do his own estate planning. All he had to do was get around to reading the book and thinking all the problems through. As a matter of fact, on the day he had his heart attack, he was wondering when he would find the time to get started.

26. *Increased Tax Due to Apportionment:* Husband drew his own will and named his wife beneficiary of half his estate and his children beneficiary of the other half. What he forgot to do was to direct the executor to pay the taxes only from those gifts that give rise to the tax. As a result, taxes were apportioned to all the beneficiaries under the terms of his will, even though wife's bequest qualified for the marital deduction and didn't give rise to any of the tax.

Unfortunately, the tax paid from her share reduced the marital deduction, which in turn increased the tax. The increased tax would again have to be apportioned to her share, which would again decrease the marital deduction and increase the tax, and around we go again until we find the balance. In the final analysis, the family had to cough up an additional 7 to 8 per cent of the estate in taxes.

27. *Election Against the Will:* Husband has three children by his first wife who died two years ago. He loved his three children and his new wife with equal fervor, and just to prove it, he named each of them beneficiary of 25 per cent of his estate. Everybody was surprised and hurt when shortly after husband's death, second wife elected against husband's will and received a one-third share. This might have been avoided in most states through the use of an inter vivos trust, had husband taken the precaution of consulting with an attorney.

28. *The Do-it-Yourself Non-Will:* Husband tore a will form out of a book that claimed he could do it himself. He filled in the blanks and being very careful, had two witnesses sign the instrument just before he signed it. The fact that one of the witnesses was his wife and the other his son didn't seem to present any serious problem to husband. After his death, when it was too late, they all found out that not only should he have signed the will first but the wife and son were limited to their intestate share under the law of his domicile. Actually, they were lucky. In some states the witness is precluded in sharing in the testator's estate at all unless the will is successfully contested.

29. *Qualified Plan Resulting in Ordinary Income:* Employee had a $200,000 interest in his company's pension plan when he retired last year. He received a lump sum payment and expected to pay the 25 per cent capital gain tax allowed for such payments on termination of employment. Unfortunately, he accepted a monthly consulting fee of $1,000, which IRS said made him an employee, therefore negating the requisite "termination." The entire $200,000 payment was taxable at ordinary income rates on top of his other income.

APPENDIX

Twenty-one Point Comparison of Five
Methods of Transferring Property to Beneficiaries

	Out-right Gift	Revoc. Trust	Private Annuity	Joint Owner	Will
1. Can executor's fee be reduced?	yes	yes	yes	yes	no
2. Can attorney's fee be reduced?	yes	yes	yes	yes	no
3. Can appraiser's fees be reduced?	yes	yes	yes	yes	no
4. Can interruption of a going business be avoided?	yes	yes	yes	yes	no
5. Can interruption of family's support be avoided?	N.A. [1]	yes	yes	yes	no
6. Can estate owner see trust in operation?	N.A.	yes	N.A.	N.A.	no
7. Can estate owner obtain lifetime management of property?	yes	yes	yes	yes	no
8. Can publicity be avoided?	yes	yes	yes	no	no
9. Can charities be assured of bequests?	yes	yes	yes	yes	no
10. Can ancillary administration be avoided?	yes	yes	yes	yes	no
11. Can publicity of accountings be avoided?	yes	yes	yes	yes	no
12. Can state inheritance taxes on insurance proceeds be avoided?	N.A.	yes	yes	yes	N.A.

189

Methods of Transferring Property to Beneficiaries (continued)

	Out-right Gift	Revoc. Trust	Private Annuity	Joint Owner	Will
13. Can estate owner be cared for if he becomes incompetent?	N.A.	yes	yes	yes	N.A.
14. Can trustee be beneficiary of life insurance?	N.A.	yes	N.A.	N.A.	N.A.
15. Can the estate owner modify the trust provisions?	N.A.	yes	no	N.A.	N.A.
16. Are assets subject to federal estate taxes?	no	yes	no	yes	yes
17. Are assets subject to gift tax?	yes	no	Q-no[2]	Q-no[3]	no
18. Are assets subject to state inheritance taxes?	no	yes	no	yes	yes
19. Do assets acquire a new cost basis at death?	no	yes	no	yes	yes
20. Can attacks on the dispositive plan be reduced?	yes	yes	yes	yes	no
21. Can estate owner choose state of jurisdiction?	yes	yes	Q-yes[4]	Q-yes[5]	no

1. N.A. = not applicable.
2. Not unless actuarial value of life income is less than value of property.
3. Creation or unwinding of joint property can be a taxable gift, but shift of ownership to survivor by death is not.
4. Qualified yes. An annuity of this type is a contract, and therefore the state of jurisdiction may be chosen.
5. By arranging initiation of the joint ownership in a particular state, for instance; naturally, one may not choose the state of jurisdiction when the property involved is real estate.

PRELIMINARY INVENTORY QUESTIONNAIRE

FAMILY DATA

1. Name   Date of Birth   Health   Insurable
    Husband
    Wife

2. Residence
    Home address
    Business address
    Present main residence -- state
    Period of residence in present state
    If less than 10 years, list prior residences:

    Any other residence or place which may be considered a residence or domicile, such as apartment or house maintained elsewhere, including summer house, voting address, church membership, club membership, etc., in other state?

3. Citizenship
    Husband: USA ( )   Other ( )
    Wife: USA ( )   Other ( )

4. Children and grandchildren

Name	Date of Birth	Married	Number of Children	Occupation *

    * Source of livelihood of married daughter, occupation of husband

5. Other dependents

Name	Date of Birth	Relationship

6. Special family problems
    Previous marriages and commitments therefrom (copy of decree and settlement papers)

    Prospective inheritances

ASSETS

Estimate the value of each of the following items of property owned by ·
you and your wife (if any) and indicate if jointly owned.

	OWNED BY		
	Husband	Wife	Jointly
A. Cash and accounts	$	$	$
B. Notes, accounts receivable, mortgages			
C. Bonds			
D. Stock			
E. Real estate:			
F. Employee benefits (bring in last statement and descriptive booklets)			
G. Stock options:			
Number of shares			
Option price			
Current value			
H. Insurance (bring policies)·			
I. Personal effects			
J. Miscellaneous property (patents, trademarks, copyrights, royalties, etc.)			
K. Business interests (bring in last balance sheet and P & L statement, tax returns, buy-sell agreements, etc.)			

LIABILITIES

A. Real estate mortgages			
B. Notes to banks			
C. Loans on insurance policies			
D. Accounts to others			
E. Pledges to churches and charities			
F. Taxes			

CHECKLIST OF DOCUMENTS AND OTHER INFORMATION NEEDED

		Received	Returned
1) Birth Certificate -- yours, spouse's, children's	1		
2) Social Security Card No. .... Marriage certificate	2		
3) Deeds to Realty	3		
4) Leases on property on which you are the lessor or lessee	4		
5) Partnership agreements	5		
6) Business agreement between yourself and associates (Redemption)	6		
7) Purchase & sale contracts	7		
8) Close corporation charters, by-laws & minute books	8		
9) Balance sheets & profit & loss statements for last 5 years, in all businesses in which you have a proprietary interest	9		
10) Personal balance sheets and income statements for last 5 years, if any were made	10		
11) Divorce decrees	11		
12) Property settlements with spouse antenuptial agreements	12		
13) Trust instruments	13		
14) Your will	14		
Spouse's will			
Will of other members of family, if pertinent			
15) Instruments creating power of appointment of which you are donee or donor	15		
16) Life insurance policies & dividend data	16		
17) General insurance policies	17		
18) Copies of employment contracts, pension benefits, etc.	18		
19) Other legal documents evidencing possible or actual rights and/or liabilities	19		
20) Income tax returns, federal & state, for past five years	20		
21) Gift tax returns and copies of revenue agent's reports if any	21		
22) Veterans service records	22		

ADVISORS

	Name	Address	Phone No.
Attorney			
Accountant			
Trust Officer			
Other bank officer			
Life Insurance Underwriter			
Investment Advisor			
Stock Broker utilized by client			
Tax Advisor			
General Insurance Broker			
Others